The Loving Care
of Pet Parrots

Rosemary Low

hancock

house

ISBN 0-88839-439-X
Copyright © 1999 Rosemary Low

Cataloging in Publication Data
Low, Rosemary.
    The loving care of pet parrots

    Includes bibliographical references and index.
    ISBN 0-88839-439-X

    1. Parrots. II. Title.
SF473.P3L68 1998   636.6'865   C98-910503-2

Editor: Nancy Miller
Production: Nancy Miller and Ingrid Luters
Cover photographs: David Hancock

Published simultaneously in Canada and the United States by

HANCOCK HOUSE PUBLISHERS LTD.
19313 Zero Avenue, Surrey, B.C. V4P 1M7
(604) 538-1114 Fax (604) 538-2262

HANCOCK HOUSE PUBLISHERS
1431 Harrison Avenue, Blaine, WA 98230-5005
(604) 538-1114 Fax (604) 538-2262
Web Site: www.hancockhouse.com *email:* sales@hancockhouse.com

Contents

Dedication

This book is dedicated to my Amazon, Lito, my companion of 30 years. She taught me how to behave around a parrot.

Acknowledgements

My thanks to Sally Blanchard for permission to quote from *Pet Bird Report*. I am also grateful to David and Vera Dennison, publishers of the South African magazine *Avizandum*, for permission to reproduce the cartoons drawn by Melanie Oliphant.

Photographs were kindly provided by Dianne Albright (pages 138 and 155), Pam Bowyer (pages 119 and 187), Lars Lepperhoff (page 37) and Val Moat (page 42). (All other photographs are by the author.) Tracy Lorriman kindly allowed me to photograph her parrots and their toys.

Introduction

The intelligence and the emotional sensitivity of parrots is enormously underestimated by most parrot keepers. The result is that many parrots suffer great cruelty unconsciously inflicted by their owners. I believe that parrots are the most misunderstood of all companion animals. To avoid this type of suffering, the owner should look at the parrot's world from his or her own perspective. In other words, bird owners must realise that they have in their care intelligent, thinking creatures with the same basic needs as humans. Most parrots are flock creatures and they have a great need for love and companionship. If a parrot is kept alone, without another of its own kind, the owner must play the role of the missing mate in providing that love and companionship. If a potential parrot owner cannot do that, then he or she should seek a less demanding pet.

I have written this book with the emphasis on loving care. I want to encourage owners of all kinds of parrots, from the smallest lovebird to the largest macaw, to obtain a better understanding of the wonderful creatures with whom they share their lives. By so doing, they will obtain much more from the relationship. But more importantly, their parrots will thrive on every level, especially the emotional one.

Chapter 1

Should you be a parrot owner?

A parrot can be the ultimate pet—a companion for life, daily bringer of joy and affection. Or it can be a noisy nuisance, unloved and unwanted. So much depends on the person caring for it—their attitude, discipline and affection. Not everyone has the necessary compassion or sense of responsibility to look after another living creature (be it human or avian); this is especially the case if that creature is a parrot. They are exceptionally sensitive and social beings and many are as demanding as a child.

Before considering the purchase of a single parrot as a companion, ask yourself why you want one. Tick the three aspects which are most important to you.

1. Colourful.
2. Able to talk.
3. Fashionable.
4. Adds to the beauty of your home.
5. Clever and intelligent.
6. An affectionate pet.
7. Enables you to understand another creature.
8. You love birds.

If you ticked more than two of the first four points, you are unlikely to possess the temperament which will make you a caring companion for a parrot. The intelligence of these birds is consistently underrated by most people who look after them. Many parrots suffer terrible cruelty unconsciously inflicted by an owner who does not understand them.

"Consciousness" is the word that comes to mind when I consider how most birds act, on a daily basis and in certain situations. Their mental faculties are much more finely tuned than the average person realises. Their actions are at times instinctive or unconscious—just as ours are—but they are capable of actions and feel emotions which are far beyond the realms of the instinctive.

In the U.S.A. there are a number of parrot behaviourists who teach owners how to discipline birds, based on their knowledge of the parrots' intelligence and emotions. Everyone who keeps these birds should be aware of the fact that interpreting their actions in an "anthropomorphic" manner (i.e., attributing to parrots emotions similar to those experienced by humans) will assist them in understanding their birds. This will help to create a happier world for them.

Obviously, the personality of the bird will vary with the species and with the individual. In addition, its previous experiences at the hands of humans will influence how it reacts to you. If you respond with love and patience and are able to correctly discipline your parrot (without ever raising your voice or your hand), he or she will become much more than a pet.

Before deciding to buy a parrot, you might need to be reminded that this is a very long-term responsibility. The smaller species have a potential life-span of 30 years and the larger ones 50 years—perhaps more. The thought should never be at the back of the mind that if a parrot is unsuited to the household it can be sold. Changing its home is a very traumatic experience for a parrot. You can liken it to a child being told that he or she will be sent to a new home. When you buy a parrot you are making a commitment to that bird, a commitment that should last its entire lifetime. That is why it is not a decision to be made lightly. Buy a parrot with the expectancy that it will become a member of the family, not part of the decor. You need to chose very carefully.

Perhaps you have seen an amusing cockatoo or macaw on the television and the thought occurred to you: What fun it would be to own a bird like that! My friends would really be impressed.

However, you need to know that for all the parrots which can be taught to show off in front of a camera, there are hundreds more that do not have this kind of temperament. There seems to be a general idea that because a parrot has been hand-reared it will invariably make a suitable pet. This is not the case. Many parrots do not make good pets; regardless of species, some just do not have the right temperament. One very caring breeder of cockatiels will not sell her hand-reared young until they are four months old. By that time she can judge their temperament and whether they will make good pets. She described two of the four young she had at the time: "...they love being cuddled and spending time with people." The other two, which had been reared in exactly the same way, were not so affectionate: "You can pick them up and they don't bite, but they will fly off at the first opportunity and sit by themselves. One of these is a terrific talker, but neither of them wants to be cuddled or played with." (Knights, 1997.)

Secondly, parrots have certain disadvantages as pets. They are extremely demanding, very loud and highly destructive. A large cage is high-priced and small cages are not acceptable. In recent years, certain fatal viral diseases have become widespread among parrots. Veterinary care for all pets can be expensive, and this is especially the case with parrots. If you cannot afford insurance for veterinary expenses, you cannot afford to keep one. If you think you can cope with these aspects, then you will probably ask:

Which species is best?
About 200 species of parrots have been kept as pets, although most of these are seldom available or not generally maintained as companion birds. Nevertheless, the range of available species is large enough to confuse anyone but an expert. Which species is best? is a question which is frequently asked. It is akin to enquiring who is the best person in a crowded room. The best for what? It all depends on the qualities for which you are searching. If you are looking for the best talker, I am likely to suggest that you buy

a cassette recorder instead! Parrots are not toys. To want one because it talks is an insult to its intelligence.

In the search for a suitable bird, one has to take into account the personality differences in individual birds and their owners. For this reason, it is impossible to answer this question in more than a general manner. However, two important points should be borne in mind. The first is that the behaviour of the individual bird, like that of a child, is mainly influenced by the guidance it receives from those caring for it. The second point is that the natural behaviour of the species cannot be changed. An explanation is necessary here. Parrots can be broadly divided into two groups. In the first group, which I shall call Group A, the pair bond between male and female is very strong. This means that when these species are kept as pets they can be very affectionate; in effect, their owner becomes their mate. Species in this group include Amazons, macaws, cockatoos and lories. The other extreme is the species in which the pair bond is not maintained throughout the year; the female is dominant in some of these species. I will call these Group B. They are not affectionate by nature. Examples are eclectus parrots, most lovebirds, ringnecks and other Asiatic (*Psittacula*) parrakeets. Although they can make interesting pets in some cases, they do not become what is often described as "cuddly tame."

Describing the advantages and disadvantages of some of the best known groups of parrots may be helpful.

GREY PARROT

Advantages   Not noisy, makes pleasant whistles; highly intelligent, excellent mimic. Group A.

Disadvantages   Nervous temperament, difficult for the inexperienced owner to understand. Shy with those it does not know. Very susceptible to feather plucking and to fits resulting from calcium deficiency (hypocalcaemia). Often difficult to persuade to accept a varied diet. Excessive feather dust.

AMAZON PARROTS

Advantages Colourful appearance. The popular species have extrovert personalities; often friendly toward strangers. Accept varied diet willingly. Some are good mimics or adept at mimicking laughter. Group A.

Disadvantages Noisy—expect regular periods of loud calls. Quite destructive. Mature males can be unreliable in their behaviour for two or three months of the year.

AFRICAN PARROTS (*Poicephalus*, includes Senegals, Meyer's and red-bellied)

Advantages   Small size—ideal for apartments and safer pets for children than larger species. They have big personalities for their size! Not as loud as larger parrots (yet voices quite harsh). Tame birds love to be handled. Less expensive to feed and house.

Disadvantages   Some have few bright colours. Difficult to classify as either Group A or Group B. Can be affectionate toward one particular person.

PIONUS PARROTS (including blue-headed)

Advantages   Smaller size than Amazons. Group A.

Disadvantages Males can be erratic and aggressive during breeding season (females more sweet tempered). Susceptible to fungal diseases such as aspergillosis, probably induced by lack of Vitamin A in the diet.

Pionus, such as this dusky, are very susceptible to fungal diseases.

CAIQUES (*Pionites* species)
Advantages Small, beautiful, exciting and unusual personalities. Group A.
Disadvantages Need a lot of fruit and can be messy; very strong-willed. Discipline is vital.

LARGE MACAWS
Advantages Beautiful, highly intelligent, responsive; can be extremely affectionate. Group A.
Disadvantages Loud, destructive and expensive to feed and house. Totally unsuitable for inexperienced owners. Can be aggressive and can bite very hard. Susceptible to feather plucking. Demanding birds which need much time devoted to them.

SMALL MACAWS
Advantages Affectionate and playful if hand-reared; like to be handled. Intelligent. Learn to repeat a few words. Group A.
Disadvantages Noisy, destructive. Susceptible to feather plucking.

CONURES
Advantages Very affectionate, playful and intelligent. Low price of some species. Moderate talking ability; excellent talking ability in the quaker parrakeet. Small size. Group A.
Disadvantages Loud voices, except Pyrrhura species such as red-bellied and green-cheeked.

PARROTLETS (*Forpus* species)
Advantages Small size, very friendly and amusing if hand-reared. Good talkers; lots of personality.
Disadvantages None. Difficult to classify as Group A or Group B.

COCKATOOS
Advantages Beautiful, affectionate and intelligent. Group A.
Disadvantages Too demanding for the average person; need much time devoted to them. Liable to become screamers and feather pluckers. Expensive to purchase and to house. Excessive feather dust. Very destructive. Please refer to further comments in Chapter 12.

COCKATIEL

Advantages   Easy to tame, affectionate, good mimic, small size, long-lived for size (up to 30 years), many colour mutations; inexpensive to purchase and to keep. Readily available. Group A.

Disadvantages   Very shrill call.

LOVEBIRDS

Advantages   Small size; inexpensive to purchase, feed and house; many colour mutations.

Disadvantages   Not tame unless hand-reared; best kept in pairs; seldom mimic; less exciting personalities than larger parrots. Susceptible to feather plucking. Difficult to classify as Group A or Group B but nearer to the latter; females dominant in some species.

LORIES AND LORIKEETS

Advantages   Beautiful, amusing, playful, very affectionate if tame. Group A.

Disadvantages   Time-consuming to clean cage and surrounding area. Larger species have harsh voices.

ECLECTUS

Advantages   Beautiful, good mimics.

Disadvantages   Seldom as affectionate as other large parrots; can be very noisy. There are exceptions, but females tend to be aggressive when mature. Group B.

AUSTRALIAN PARRAKEETS

Advantages   None.

Disadvantages   Hand-reared birds become aggressive with maturity. Group B.

Not everyone will agree with the above assessments! As I said, they are generalisations and not rules. Parrots' personalities and abilities vary as much as do those of humans. Remember, of course, that if you buy a young bird, whatever the species, you can teach discipline. An older bird may have been ill-treated or neglected and, at least initially, will be much less responsive.

Species such as ringnecks and Australian parrakeets are seldom kept as pets. They are not usually affectionate toward their owner and are more suited to life in an aviary. Unfortunately, in recent years there has been a trend toward hand-rearing species which are unsuitable as pets to make them easier to sell. This includes kakarikis and rosellas. Do not be persuaded that such birds make suitable pets, because this is definitely not the case.

One bird or two?
Parrots are supremely sociable creatures. You might be tempted to keep one although you know you really do not have the time available to do justice to its emotional needs. A neglected parrot becomes a sad feather plucker or screamer whose life is without pleasure. Parrots of the species most often kept as pets have a deep need for a permanent relationship, either with a human or with a bird of their own species. This is why these species have become such popular companion birds: they have so much affection to give. If you know in your heart you do not have the time to make a parrot happy, you might consider buying an unrelated young pair and keeping them in a large indoor aviary (if the species is suitable) or in an outdoor aviary. In due course they should breed. Perhaps by then your circumstances may have changed and you can take one of the young ones and make it into the pet you always wanted. For the birds, the main benefit is that they are never without a companion and playmate. This means that they will be emotionally much less demanding from your point of view.

Chapter 2

Choice of species

No two parrot individuals are alike but each species has certain characteristics. This chapter is intended as a general guide to these characteristics. It is important to remember that generalisations are unwise where parrots are concerned! Also, the behaviour of an individual will be influenced by its previous experiences of man.

Amazon Parrots

Although one Amazon, a yellow-front, has been my companion for more than 30 years, I cannot unreservedly recommend Amazons as pets. If bird and owner are well matched, it is a marriage made in heaven; if not, it's a nightmare! Of course, on purchase of a young bird, it is seldom possible to assess compatibility. Amazons do have strong likes and dislikes where people are concerned; often there is a bias toward men or women. Incidentally, the popular conception of parrots preferring people of the opposite sex to themselves is not true.

Three of the most popular Amazon species have a very excitable temperament. I would not consider males to be safe pets where there are children in the household. These are blue-fronted (*Amazona aestiva*), double yellow-head (*Amazona o. oratrix*) and yellow-naped (*Amazona auropalliata*). The spectacled or white-fronted (*Amazona albifrons*) is more suitable, for its small size, and some yellow-fronted or yellow-crowned (*Amazona o. ochrocephala*) have a less excitable temperament. Amazons have regular periods of screaming, usually in the morning, thus will not be suitable in some households.

Asiatic Parrakeets

The Indian ringneck (*Psittacula krameri manillensis*) is the only species widely offered as a pet. This has happened since the great popularity of the many mutations; some breeders hand-rear some young to sell as pets, to widen the market. While it is true that these intelligent birds can make excellent pets, they need to be with someone who can spend a lot of time with them. If they are not handled frequently, at least daily, they will lose their tameness. This is not a species for someone who wants a "cuddly tame" parrot. However, because of the low price it may be the only one, apart from the cockatiel, which many people can afford. If they have plenty of time to devote to it, and allow it to fly about the house daily, it will make an attractive pet and possibly a wonderful talker. If not, it is cruel to keep it in a pet situation, especially with clipped wings. These active birds need to be able to fly—preferably in an aviary.

Cockatiel

A hand-reared cockatiel, or a parent-reared young one, obtained as soon as it is independent, is the perfect pet for most families.

The only disadvantage is the shrill voice which carries a long way. Cockatiels are long-lived and can become superb talkers. They are available in countless colour mutations and combinations.

Cockatoos

The best word of advice I can give regarding their purchase is: Don't! I could qualify this to say: Don't—unless you are a very experienced parrot keeper and you can devote several hours to one bird daily. If you cannot, you will almost certainly end up with a

Young cockatoos look adorable. In fact, few birds are more difficult and demanding.

screaming, feather-plucking cockatoo. I advise people against buying cockatoos as pets—not because I do not like these birds, but because they are terribly misunderstood. It is heart-breaking to see the result. Cockatoos are among the most intelligent and sensitive of all birds. They deserve better than to spend most of their lives in a cage. They are also highly sociable and crave the companionship of their own species. If you want to keep a cockatoo and you do not have any close neighbours, build an aviary and buy a young pair.

Grey Parrot

If properly disciplined and with a caring owner, greys obtained young make wonderful pets. They do not need to be hand-reared; indeed parent-reared birds may be less demanding and easier to live with as they mature. Their talent for mimicry is legendary and well deserved.

Lories and Lorikeets

A few of the medium and large-sized species make wonderful pets; the best are probably the green-naped (*Trichoglossus h. haematodus*), the dusky (*Pseudeos fuscata*), yellow-backed and chattering (*Lorius g. flavopalliatus* and *L. g. garrulus*) and the black-capped (*Lorius lory*). However, the *Lorius* species can be very noisy. In all lories, the liquid droppings are a major disadvantage which create work. In the U.S.A., lories have been promoted as pets by persuading purchasers that they can be kept on a dry, powdered food, thus producing more solid faeces. In my opinion, this food should account for no more than 30 percent of the diet in, for example, green-naped lorikeets and dusky lories. The more nectivorous species would die if offered nothing else. They all need a liquid food manufactured especially for them, obtained in powder form. Lories and lorikeets will be kept successfully as house pets only by the real enthusiasts. They will need to place plastic matting around the cage and the wall near it should have a washable surface—either tiles or a washable wall covering. The larger lories also have loud or shrill voices. Anyone who can overlook these faults will have a colourful, playful and affectionate pet which is quite unlike any other parrot—and a never-ending source of amusement. As my opinion might be considered to show a strong bias toward these lovely birds, let me quote another source: "The brilliant intelligence found in lories is both a blessing and a challenge.

"The lories' intelligence makes them happier birds; they always seem to find something with which to entertain themselves. I have never heard of a healthy, properly fed lory picking its feathers from boredom. In many ways, I consider them the perfect career family pet. They can amuse themselves while their owners are gone and be in a perfectly cheery mood when their owners return home.... The challenging aspect of their intelligence is that what they want to play with isn't always what you want them to play with! I have seen lories stretch their feet out through the bars of their cage to amazing distances to snag something that caught their eye, be it a plant, a child's toy, an electric cord or, in one case, the pet Labrador's tail!" (Sefton, 1995/6.)

Macaws

The large species should be considered only by experienced parrot owners. Newcomers do not have the knowledge to deal with the many facets of large macaw ownership.

Blue and Yellow Macaw (Ara ararauna)

The species most often kept as a pet. Young hand-reared birds are irresistible. Unfortunately, this often leads to them being obtained on impulse by people who have neither the time nor the experience to keep them. As a result, it is not uncommon to see severely feather plucked examples. This is the most suitable species for someone who fulfils the necessary criteria for large macaw ownership. They are readily available, commonly bred and less expensive than other large macaws. They are affectionate and playful, very intelligent and observant.

Green-winged Macaw (Ara chloroptera)

A suitable species for the experienced parrot owner who is not intimidated by the large size and large beak. Most green-wings obtained as hand-fed youngsters have wonderful temperaments and are highly intelligent. This would be my choice of the more available species. Females especially are extremely affectionate and sweet natured.

Military Macaw (Ara militaris)

Young hand-reared birds make loving and amusing pets in sympathetic hands. They are often underrated and with an undeserved reputation for not making good pets. They are friendly and outgoing.

The following species are on Appendix 1 of CITES, i.e., they are endangered. The scarlet (Ara macao), Buffon's (Ara ambigua), blue-throated (Ara glaucogularis) and the hyacinthine (Anodorhynchus hyacinthinus) are not bred in large enough numbers in Europe to place them on the pet market. Although larger numbers are reared in the U.S.A., there should be more emphasis on using most of these birds for breeding purposes. Almost 100 percent are being hand-reared for the pet trade.

Macaws which have been weaned gradually and not forced-weaned, especially females, are sweet-tempered and affectionate. However, scarlets do not respond well to being challenged, be it from a human or another bird. Then they are liable to become aggressive. It is a very unwise and unsympathetic person who uses physical violence against a scarlet macaw. It is unthinkable to treat any bird in this way....

Red-fronted Macaw (Ara rubrogenys)

A medium-sized macaw, endangered and on Appendix 1 of CITES. Perhaps the day will come when its captive numbers have increased sufficiently to allow some to be released for the pet market. In fact, its smaller size and pleasant temperament make it an excellent pet.

Small Macaws (sometimes called mini-macaws)

Illiger's macaw (Ara maracana) is endangered and on Appendix 1 of CITES. At the present time more young birds should be set up for breeding rather than placed as pets. The red-bellied macaw (Ara manilata) does not do well in captivity; it is very prone to obesity and should not be closely confined as a pet. If it is, its life will be short.

The other small macaws, in descending order of size, are the severe (*Ara severa*), yellow-collared (*Ara auricollis*), noble (*Diopsittaca* or *Ara nobilis cumanensis*) and Hahn's (*D.* or *A. nobilis nobilis*). They all make fantastic pets. They are intelligent, amusing, very playful and extremely affectionate. My own choice would be the yellow-collared. They can be quite loud but if one overlooks this fault they are almost perfect pets. I rate small macaws higher than Amazons, except for the person for whom talking ability is important. Some are good mimics, however.

Parrotlets

Imagine the form of an Amazon parrot scaled down to about 13 cm (5 in) in length, but with a shorter tail, and you have a parrotlet (*Forpus* species). Its voice is proportionately small. To anyone looking for a small parrot, but "something different," I would recommend a hand-reared parrotlet. Where space is at a premium they are ideal. Parrotlets may be the pet parrot of the future. Their extraordinary talking ability, quiet calls and the increasing number of colour mutations will add to their popularity. They are easy to look after and young birds readily accept a pelleted diet. However, they do not seem to realise how small they are and will not hesitate to try to dominate larger birds, such as a cockatiel. If they try this with even larger species they could be in trouble.

The small *Poicephalus* parrots make excellent pets. Seen here are young birds of two species, red-bellied (left) and Senegal (right).

Pionus

Blue-headed (*P. menstruus*), Maximilian's (*P. maximiliani*) and the small white-crowned (*P. senilis*) are most likely to be available as pets. Their temperament varies. I have seen delightfully sweet and affectionate birds, also one which was spiteful and aggressive. I would not recommend them for a household where children cannot be trusted not to annoy them.

Poicephalus

The smaller African parrots, such as the Senegal (*P. senegalus*), Meyer's (*P. meyeri*), brown-headed (*P. cryptoxanthus*) and red-bellied (*P. rufiventris*) make adorable pets if obtained when young. The slightly larger Jardine's (*P. gulielmi*) can also make a superb pet: a playful extrovert. The rare and endangered Cape parrot (*P. robustus*) should be available only to serious breeders (who will not hand-rear them if they wish to help conserve this species in aviculture). Despite their small size, the small *Poicephalus* are very strong-willed birds that need a lot of attention. All species can become accomplished mimics. Some become extremely attached to one person to the exclusion of all others.

Quaker Parrakeet

This 29 cm (11 in) long parrakeet (*Myiopsitta monachus*) is free-breeding and inexpensive. Hand-reared birds often make adorable pets and some are excellent mimics. The voice is loud and harsh—but some hand-reared birds are less noisy.

Male or female?

If you have a choice, should you choose a male or a female? This choice will be dependent on several factors. As explained in Chapter 1, parrots can be approximately classified into two groups. In Group A the pair bond is strong; in this group both sexes should make affectionate pets. In Group B the pair bond is not maintained throughout the year and females may be dominant. Given the choice, in Group B I would choose a male as a pet. In Group A, I would prefer a female. This is because when males come into breeding condition they can be aggressive and, frankly, dangerous. This often applies to large macaws and some Amazons, especially blue-fronts and double yellow-heads. In my experience with lories, tame females remain extremely affectionate and loving, whereas males are more liable to nip as they mature. Male greys are more likely to try to dominate members of the household (or the entire household!) than are females.

Modern technology has brought certain important advances for parrot breeders. Not only can birds be sexed before they mature, they can be sexed in nest feather! The first method of positively identifying sex in monomorphic species (those in which plumage is alike in male and female) was surgical sexing. This started in the 1970s. The main disadvantages are that the bird must be anaesthetised (bringing the risk of death caused by anaesthetic) and the comparatively high rate of inaccurate results. This is an invasive method, in other words, an incision is made in the bird's side and an endoscope is inserted to view the testes or ovaries. These days noninvasive sexing methods are preferred by most people. Using DNA found in blood or feathers, all widely-kept parrot species can be sexed. No special skill is needed to remove three or four feathers from the breast. The bird should be held firmly in a towel and the appropriate feather should be grasped with a pair of tweezers in the centre of the feather, near the base. A quick sharp tug will remove the feather. The sample is sent off to the laboratory in a special envelope and the results are available one to four days after receipt. In the U.K., this service costs about £20 for a single bird in 1998 and in the U.S.A. it costs about $20. Anyone buying from a breeder could pay extra to have the chosen young bird sexed before it is even weaned. In this way they would know that they were buying a parrot of the preferred sex. Alternatively, some breeders do this in advance as an incentive to buy.

Many young hand-reared parrots, such as these greys, are ordered from a breeder, perhaps even before they hatch. The buyer may be permitted to visit the young parrot before the day of purchase.

Chapter 3

Where you can buy your bird

Do not be in a hurry to buy! If well cared for, your parrot could be with you for decades! Don't buy on impulse!

Countless parrots suffer mental torture by being sold or passed on over and over again. This happens because many people do not give sufficient thought to whether they really want a parrot or whether the bird they are buying is right for them. I was told about an umbrella cockatoo which had had seven homes in four months. That experience must have been psychological torture for the cockatoo. Why had this happened? Because the cockatoo screamed a lot.

The screaming no doubt became worse, out of fear and insecurity. All healthy cockatoos scream—and anyone who cannot tolerate this or does not have the time to make their cockatoo so contented that screaming is minimal, should not contemplate the purchase of such a sensitive bird. However, the purchaser is not always to blame. Sometimes it is the seller's fault for selling a young bird which has been force-weaned or which has not been handled enough to make a good pet. Or the seller may not have told the truth about the bird's abilities.

After studying the list of advantages and disadvantages of the various species, visit a bird park, zoo or specialist bird shop where a good selection of parrot species is available. In this way you may encounter a species which particularly attracts you.

If it is within your financial means, but not for sale when you see it, look through the advertisements in an avicultural magazine or visit a pet store which sells captive-bred birds. A large store is likely to have a better choice. A store which obtains all their young birds from one source is generally preferable. The disease risk when young birds from various breeders are introduced to each other at a young age (before their immune systems are fully functional) is high.

If you search through the advertisements in avicultural magazines you may be surprised at the different prices at which the same species are offered. For example, in 1998 young grey parrots were being offered for around £250 or for between £450 and £500 in the U.K. Although the information was not given in the advertisements, those offered at £250 were wild-caught birds. Many purchasers were unaware of this fact. They were also unaware that the death rate in wild-caught greys during the first three months or so after they are released from quarantine (a 35-day period in the U.K.) is very high. No breeder would sell a captive-bred bird for less than £450, except a Timneh grey, which is worth slightly less.

This might seem high in comparison with wild-caught birds. In fact it is not. In 1995, a friend who specialised in breeding greys worked out exactly what it cost to rear one bird, taking all expenses into account. The answer was £450. Very few small breeders make any money and many operate at a loss. In the U.S. only captive-bred birds are available. They range from $400 to $1,000 each.

When you are studying the advertisements you may see some abbreviations. The most relevant ones are HR for hand-reared, CB for captive-bred or AB for aviary-bred. (The term domestically bred is used in the U.S.A.) CY means current year and SS means surgically sexed. In the case of pairs, U/R means unrelated. Hatch certificate is a document showing date of hatching, breeder and identification (ring or microchip). It does not mean that the bird's details have been registered anywhere. If the bird ever goes to a new home, this certificate should accompany it.

Although you may be tempted by the lower price of a wild-caught bird, you must realise the following. By patronising dealers who trade in such birds you are contributing to the death of several other birds. For each wild-caught bird which survives to be exported, several or even many more have died. In some countries, such as the U.S.A., trade in wild-caught birds is illegal and mass importation has ceased. In some other countries, such as Australia and New Zealand, only a very small and limited number of birds are permitted to enter the country each year. They are imported through government quarantine stations and are either captive-bred or wild-caught birds which have been many years in captivity.

It is advisable to locate a bird within travelling distance of your home; on no account buy a parrot unseen. It may be sick, untameable, unsuitable or it may even take a dislike to you! Parrots are as individualistic as humans; unlike a dog they will not attach themselves to anyone who showers them with affection. Even a young hand-reared bird, just weaned, is quite likely to show an immediate bias. An older bird, which has already had an owner, will probably show a strong preference for a man or for a woman. That preference may become apparent within minutes of introduction. If he doesn't like you then, perhaps he never will! On introduction, don't be overfamiliar! And don't expect too much at that first meeting. Watch the bird quietly for a minute or two before approaching it. Talk to it quietly and keep your hands away from the cage if the bird is not hand-reared. The close proximity of hands may make some parrots frightened or aggressive.

With a young hand-reared bird you take a different approach. It will be longing for attention and just waiting to climb all over you. Spend at least ten minutes watching it. While you are observing, look for signs of good health.

GOOD HEALTH	POOR HEALTH
Eyes bright	Eyes dull or frequently closed; discharge from eyes or nostrils
Active, alert and periodically preening	Lethargic
Vent clean	Faeces around vent or even trailing
Clean beak	Food stuck to beak, vomiting or retching
Beak normal length and shape	Overgrown beak indicative of aged bird or one with a liver disease; misshapen beak in hand-reared bird suggests rickets—examine bones (see below)

Good body condition	Poor body weight—breast bone prominent (need to handle bird to discover this)
Bones in legs and wings straight	Crooked or bowed legs indicative of rickets (calcium deficiency), also wings hanging down
Plumage complete and glossy	Plumage dull, with blackish areas; blood quills or feathers partly retained in sheath; areas bare of feathers indicative of feather plucking or PBFD*
Plumage held sleek to body	Plumage fluffed out, especially when bird is sleeping
Apparently normal faeces	Apparently abnormal faeces, e.g., too much white, abnormal colour not associated with food eaten, undigested food** or blood (red or blackish) in faeces
Unbroken skin on feet	Flaky skin or raw reddish skin on underside of centre of foot (indicative of Vitamin A deficiency—this is treatable)
Nails normal length	Overgrown nails might suggest aged bird

*Psittacine beak and feather disease, an incurable condition which causes feather loss and, in cockatoos, abnormal beak growth. See Chapter 18.

**A common symptom in birds suffering from PDD. See Chapter 18.

It is often stated that a healthy bird sleeps on one leg with its head tucked into the feathers of its back. However, this statement needs qualifying. Very young and very old birds that are healthy often sleep on both legs and sick birds sometimes sleep on only one leg.

If the bird that you are considering with interest passes this test of outward signs of good health and it seems to like you, you are all set to make the big decision. Ask the sales assistant for more information about the bird. If he or she tells you something which you doubt, do not be afraid to question the statement. Unfortunately some assistants are not well informed and others may tell you anything to sell a bird that no-one is interested in.

If you see a young parrot that takes your eye, watch it quietly for a minute or two before approaching it. These two Jardine's parrots were playful and active.

One lady was told that it is better to buy a male parrot because you can recoup the cost by "putting it out to stud." This is obviously rubbish. Parrots do not mate on introduction. It usually takes months or years!

It is so easy to be tempted into an unwise purchase in a store. My advice is to go away for an hour; do some shopping or have a cup of coffee. Discuss the purchase with your partner or with a friend. Telephone anyone you know who keeps parrots. If you buy an unsuitable bird, it will suffer, you will suffer and so, possibly, will the relationship with your partner. Alternatively, place a small deposit which the owner might refund if you give your answer in 24 hours. On the spur of the moment it is sometimes difficult to say "no"—but "no" might be the right answer.

Unfortunately, many purchasers are given incorrect information about the age of the bird. Judging by letters I have received from disappointed buyers, this aspect is the one that is most likely to be wrong. The reason is simple: pet shop owners know that purchasers are looking for a young bird, also that it is more difficult to sell an older one. There are many honest sellers who can be trusted but, unfortunately, there are also many dishonest ones. Be wary of a seller who gives such information as: "It will only take two months to teach him to talk." It is impossible to judge the potential of individual birds. They vary. The honest seller might point out that there is no guarantee that ANY bird will talk.

How to recognise a young bird

In some popular species, young birds are easily distinguished by the eye colour, that is, the iris. The pupil is black in all parrots. The table below shows the colour of the iris in young birds, that of adults, and the approximate age when adult eye colour is attained.

EYE COLOUR AND CHARACTERISTICS OF YOUNG BIRDS

Species: blue and yellow macaw*
Immature: grey—soon becoming yellow-grey
Adult: pale yellow
Age: yellow at 18 months but not as light as adult

*All very young macaws have shorter tails than adults.

Species: blue-fronted Amazon
Immature: grey-brown
Adult: orange
Age: five months

Species: blue-headed pionus
Immature: dark
Adult: dark-brown
Age: n/a
(young have duller plumage; some birds have red frontal band; pale lower mandible and pale sides to upper mandible)

Species: double yellow-headed Amazon
Immature: grey-brown
Adult: orange
Age: five months
(also note head coloration: yellow confined to forehead and crown; takes five or six years for head to become mainly yellow)

Species: dusky lory
Immature: brownish
Adult: orange
Age: four months

Species: green-winged macaw
Immature: greyish
Adult: pale yellow
Age: about 18 months
(lower mandible partly light coloured in birds under about six months)

Species: grey parrot
Immature: grey
Adult: yellow
Age: 12 to 18 months

Species: Hahn's macaw
Immature: grey-brown
Adult: orange
Age: reddish-brown by about five months

Species: Jardine's parrot
Immature: greyish
Adult: red-brown
Age: 12 to 18 months
(head dusky-brown, little or no orange on forehead; in very young birds the cere is pink and the base of the upper mandible is light)

Species: Senegal parrot
Immature: black, then grey, then yellow-grey
Adult: yellow
Age: 12 to 18 months
(beak has pink at base of upper mandible in very young birds; plumage much duller until first moult at about one year)

Species: lovebirds
Immature: dark
Adult: dark

Age: n/a
(young have dark tip to beak and paler plumage; adult appearance attained at five months)

Species: yellow-collared macaw
Immature: greyish brown at 3½ months
Adult: reddish brown
Age: about six months

Species: yellow-fronted (yellow-crowned) Amazon
Immature: greyish brown
Adult: orange
Age: about six months

Note that in species where the iris is orange or yellow, this colour is acquired quite early but the full intensity of eye colour takes perhaps another year or more to acquire.

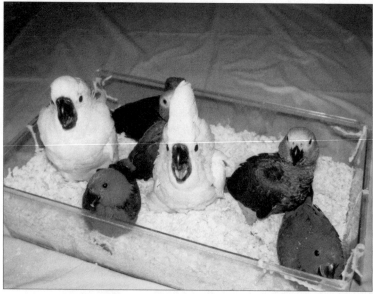

Species such as grey and eclectus parrots and Moluccan cockatoos are hand-reared for the pet trade.

This female eclectus (*vosmaeri*) is identified as a young bird by her dark eye and by the brown marks on the dull-coloured beak.

These days many hand-reared parrots are ordered from a breeder soon after they hatch. The prospective purchaser is permitted to visit his or her bird as it grows. An initial deposit will be requested. This method of buying is often used for popular pet species such as greys or Amazons. The buyer is mentally preparing for weeks for the day on which he or she brings the bird home. There is also plenty of time to make the practical preparations such as saving and shopping for cage and toys.

This is an excellent way of buying a young parrot. Contact a cage bird magazine or avicultural society. The secretary should be able to put you in touch with a parrot breeder.

Guidelines for sellers

If you do not merely sell birds but give a good service, your good reputation will grow. One breeder could be considered to be a model seller. She provided the following with each young bird: hatch certificate, photograph of the bird as a chick, a pamphlet describing basic care, information on the species, leaflets from

31

manufacturers of pellets, a brochure from a local bird behaviourist and the parrot's favourite toy.

Local newspapers and auctions

Another method of finding a parrot is to read the classified advertisements of local newspapers. There are, of course, genuine reasons for sale in some cases, such as the birth of a baby or feather allergy. But in many other instances the bird is being sold because it bites or it screams. This is probably not the bird's fault—and in experienced hands it could become a rewarding pet. However, first-time buyers are warned against such purchases, even though the price may be temptingly low. It is unlikely that they could cope with them.

Suppose, however, that a friend has a tame parrot which he or she can no longer keep. It may be one which you have known and admired for a long time. Is it a good idea to buy an older bird? There is absolutely no reason why it should not make a wonderful pet, if you give it abundant love and care. Its age is not important, neither is the fact that it has had a previous owner. The myth that older birds will not give their heart to a new owner can be ignored. However, it is wise to find out, if possible, whether the parrot has a preference for men or for women. One should also be prepared for the fact that it may take longer for the bond between bird and owner to be established than with a recently weaned parrot. But winning the trust of an older bird can be very rewarding indeed.

Another option is buying from a bird auction. Breeders might dispose of young birds of common and inexpensive species to auctions but it is highly unlikely that large parrots such as greys, Amazons and macaws would be for sale. If they are, there is a strong possibility that they have been stolen. If you buy a stolen bird, you could be charged with possessing stolen goods. Remember that these days many owners have their parrots microchipped. This means that positive identification of individual birds can occur.

SOURCE	ADVANTAGE	DISADVANTAGE
Private breeder	Sharing breeder's knowledge; after-sales advice often available; age of bird known	Smaller choice of birds
Pet shop or dealer	Wider choice of birds	Advice on care not always given; prices usually higher, also disease risk; history of older birds unknown
Bird auction	Lower prices	Risk of buying stolen or smuggled birds; high disease risk; no advice on care or knowledge of individual birds
Newspaper advert	Possibly lower prices	Bird may not be tame, has behavioural problem or has even been mistreated

Bill of sale

Regardless of where you buy your bird, ask for a descriptive bill of sale. It might state "Hand-reared Grey Parrot." As an extreme example, someone who knows nothing about parrots might be unable to distinguish between a hand-reared bird and a wild-caught "growler." Even if he discovered his mistake the very next day and returned the bird, if he had only a till receipt, he would not be in a strong position. With a descriptive bill of sale, the law is on his side. Also be aware that it is a legal necessity to prove your bird's origin if you move from country to country or even state to state.

Chapter 4

The cage and the stand

Good pet stores stock a wide range of cages of excellent design. It is advisable to visit a large store as their stock will be larger. In 1999, one could expect to pay as much as the bird for a cage of adequate design, depending on the size of the parrot for which it was intended. Larger cages or more ornate ones could cost very much more. If you have had a win on the lottery, you can even buy (in the U.S.A.) a cage with air filtration, acrylic dust guards, full spectrum lighting and stainless steel bars! The United States has a massive pet industry and produces probably the best thought-out cages in the world, although many Italian designs are also good. For example, in the USA there is a cage designed especially for grey parrots. In one corner is a small shelf, with solid walls, to which a bird can retire. It incorporates a removable playpen and toy holder.

There is no advantage in an ornate cage; size and good design are the most important aspects. The most common mistake made by people who are buying a parrot is to choose a cage which is too small. By law in the U.K., a bird must be kept in a cage which allows it to extend both wings. This is the minimum requirement. In actual fact such a cage would be too small. Here are some guidelines to choosing a cage:

1. In many cages, the maximum measurement is vertical; but it is length, not height, which is most important. The exception is a macaw cage; these birds need extra height above their head and depth for the long tail.

2. Do not buy a cage which has vertical bars. While this would be suitable for a canary, for example, a parrot needs to climb. It will slide up and down, not climb, if the bars are vertical.

3. The cage should be easy to clean.
4. A cage on a stand or on castors is recommended, except in the case of a small cage which is intended for a table.
5. Look for design features which may interest you, such as a cage in which part of the roof lifts up, with a perch attached; in effect, this is a cage and small stand in one.
6. The food and water containers must be removed from outside. It is very bad design if you have to put your hand inside as even some of the tamest birds resent intrusion into their territory.
7. If you have a cockatoo, look for a cage with a cockatoo-proof latch, as they can open most ordinary doors.
8. If you want to keep the area surrounding the cage clean, look for a cage with an "apron" built into the design. This catches debris.
9. Many parrot cages, especially the smaller ones, have a detachable plastic base. This is an advantage in the case of a bird which is not easily persuaded to enter the cage after a period of freedom. If he is let out at night, detach the cage from the base, note his location, turn out the light and place the cage over the bird! It can also be useful when spraying a bird inside his cage, if the cage is small. It can stand in the sink, with the bird inside.

A cage for a cockatoo should have a door that is very difficult to open. It may be necessary to screw the food and water containers to the side of the cage and use an acrylic holder, as seen right.

Here I would like to reiterate the importance of a spacious cage. Large cages are expensive and because the bird may also be high-priced, an attempt to reduce the cost is made by buying a cage which is too small for the species. Look at it this way: your bird will, hopefully, spend many years in this cage. To buy a spacious one will cost perhaps one or two pence more per day. For the pleasure he will give you, he is surely worth that. If you cannot afford a large cage, you cannot afford a parrot.

The purchaser of a bird that has not been hand-reared, especially a wild-caught cockatoo, should be aware of this fact. Nervous birds feel very threatened by close confinement in a small cage, because they cannot move far away from a threatening object (a person). Their fear turns to aggression. The same bird in a spacious cage or indoor flight could behave in a totally different and nonaggressive manner.

Location

A kitchen is not a safe place for a parrot (see Chapter 16). The best room is where he will have most company. However, the location should not be near a television set (or in the same room, if the room is small) or a gas fire or any other kind of heater. If the cage is near a window, the window should have blinds so that your parrot is never in direct sunlight. This can raise the temperature to the degree that your bird is extremely uncomfortable or even threatened by heat stress. Heat stress can kill. My own Amazon has an intense dislike of sun. On one occasion I left her on her stand; it was early evening and after a while the sun came out. She was directly in its rays. She must have been there about 15 minutes and during this time she was so uncomfortable that she plucked her breast feathers—something she had never done before.

A conservatory can be a dangerous place for a parrot because there is no escape from the sun—unless a section of the roof is covered with a blind or with shade cloth. Also remember that if your parrot is visible to passers-by, there is a risk of theft. A window that looks on to your property and not on to the street is the safest place.

36

Cages for large macaws

The large species of macaw feel uncomfortable in a cage or aviary which lacks height. An ideal macaw aviary would be at least 3 m (10 ft.) high and an ideal macaw cage would allow at least 61 cm (2 ft.) of headroom. Unfortunately, large pet cages are very expensive—but a handyman could make a superb large cage from 10-gauge 3 in. x 1 in. welded mesh at a fraction of the price. Its appearance would be less decorative—but the needs of the macaw should come first.

Cages for pet lories

Many people are attracted to lories and lorikeets as house pets but have been told they make too much mess. While this is true, you can take steps to minimise the inconvenience. Acrylic can be screwed to the sides of the cage so that droppings are mainly contained within. The area behind the cage could be tiled, or covered in a washable wall covering; as a temporary measure, heavy plastic could be used to cover the wall. Lengths of clear plastic carpet protector can be used in the vicinity of the cage. Alternatively, buy a large mynah cage; a cage 1 m (3 ft. 3 in.) long

x 50 cm (20 in.) wide x 50 cm (20 in.) high is available. This will contain most of the liquid faeces.

A flight cage

If you have a pair of birds you might consider the construction of a small flight. The framework can be made from aluminium angle, to which welded mesh is attached. You

This pair of Senegals have a home-made cage on a wooden base. Fresh branches, cardboard rolls and pieces of wood threaded on a string indicate a caring owner. It could be argued, however, that if the cage had been mounted horizontally, the Senegals would have had more flying space.

could have one made or buy the panels and erect it yourself. The resulting flight is of neat appearance and if the surrounding walls are tiled, the whole area will look attractive. A friend turned an unused utility room, off the kitchen, into a home for two pairs of birds, each with a flight 1.8 m (6 ft.) long, 91 cm (3 ft.) wide and 1.8 m (6 ft.) high. The walls and floor were tiled and the end result was superb.

There is simply no limit to a parrot aviary built as an integral part of the house, if space and finance permit. In the U.S.A., one macaw owner built a room/cage off the dining room. Patio doors were replaced by stainless steel bars, incorporating a door. The cage could be entered from the dining room or from sliding glass doors outside. The dining room entrance was framed with curtains and pelmet, like a French window. The birds could look into the house or out into the garden. On the outside a pull down blind was used for shade and for security at night.

Stands

Stands for birds (as opposed to stands for cages) come in many designs, and the most elaborate are called play-gyms. Stands are mainly used to give birds whose wings have been clipped an area away from the cage. They are easily portable so can be moved from room to room with their owner, if desired, whereas a large cage is more difficult to move. A stand helps to relieve the monotony of always seeing the same view and gives the bird a relief from looking at bars. When a parrot is outside its cage, its owner cannot always be holding it, but he or she can supervise its actions, while doing chores, such as washing the dishes, if the parrot is on his stand. My Amazon, always full-winged, will remain on her stand for some time, before climbing down to investigate or flying off. However, most full-winged parrots would not remain on a stand for long. Hers is most useful when she loudly demands to be let out when I have guests for dinner. She will become quiet as soon as she is placed on the stand. Currently she has a tabletop model, which weighs only 3 kg (7 lb.). It is much more convenient than the full-length versions of the past. These were home-made and very inexpensive. One version was made by fill-

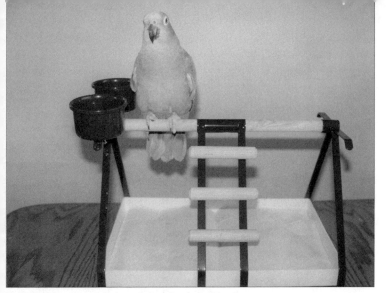

A table-top stand is used by the author's yellow-fronted Amazon.

ing a plastic plant pot with concrete and setting a carefully select-ed branch in the middle! For another, I bought a second-hand coffee table, had a hole made in the centre and set a branch in it. (When you move house overseas a throw-away type is best!)

Of course, the commercially produced types look best. Many designs are available. They have a tray to catch droppings and food, and most are on castors. Some incorporate several perches, even orthopaedic ones. In the U.S.A., there are even stands with collapsible bases, like a camera tripod. The height is adjustable and they can be folded up and placed in a bag.

Some years ago leg chains were used to confine parrots to a stand. This was a barbaric practice which resulted in many birds breaking their legs or suffering other accidents.

Perches

The quality of perches in purchased cages varies. In some, the wood is very hard and almost indestructible except by the larger species. In time these perches may become shiny with wear and difficult to grip. They should then be replaced by branches from suitable trees, such as apple. The bark will immediately be removed by the occupant; parrots love bark and it may have ben-eficial qualities. For a while the barkless perch will be rough where the bird has gnawed at it; soon it becomes hard and even-

39

tually slippery. Frequent renewal is therefore essential. At least one perch in the cage should be gnawable. The perches should have different diameters to provide foot exercise, so that the toes are not always clenched in the same position. A perch does not have to be round! The six-sided ones with the widest surface top and bottom are excellent. A trip to a large pet store will reveal a range of concrete perches which have a slightly rough surface which is very efficient in wearing the nails down slightly and removing the sharp tip to the nail. They can be screwed on to the side of the cage with the wing-nut supplied. They come in a range of colours; avoid the white ones, or dye them with fruit juice or the juice of blackberries or elder berries. I recommend these perches highly. They are indestructible (except perhaps to macaws and cockatoos) and can be positioned anywhere.

Floor surface
What should you put in the cage tray to catch the droppings? Newspaper is the best floor covering, in my opinion. Sand and shavings make a mess and could end up in the food and water. If your parrot tears up the newspaper, it does not matter—in fact, the bird is probably enjoying this activity. However, if it makes such a mess with the paper you cannot tolerate it any more, you can leave the tray bare. But it will need to be washed once or twice daily, depending on the temperature of the room and the size of the bird.

A new cage
Many parrots are very attached to their cage and will not take kindly to a replacement, when this becomes necessary. The change can be made gradually, and therefore more acceptably, if the new cage becomes a familiar object. First place it at a distance in the same room, then gradually move it closer. Place a tempting item of food or a fresh branch inside so that your parrot becomes curious and wants to enter. After he has entered a couple of times, shut the door and remove the old cage.

Chapter 5

The day of purchase

The day of purchase is a time of great excitement. The first task is to prepare the cage. It is not a good idea to buy it on the day. Your parrot should not have to wait in the carrier while you set up the cage or decide the best position. Place the food and water inside and make sure everything is ready; you should not have to put your hand inside after placing the bird there. For a nervous bird this is the worst kind of intrusion when all it wants is to settle down after a possibly frightening journey.

Unless you prepare yourself beforehand, you may arrive home with your bird and realise you have forgotten to ask many important questions. Think carefully about what you will need to know and, if necessary, make a list of questions for the seller. If the parrot has just been weaned, you need to know exactly on what he has been fed and in what kind of food containers. In his new home everything will be unfamiliar. If the food containers look the same and are located in the same position in the cage, this will encourage him to feed.

When you go to collect him, make a mental note of these points. Also, if he had a cage to himself, look at the consistency of his droppings so that you know what is normal for this particular bird. If he is a hand-reared parrot who has just been weaned, it is advisable to continue to hand feed him for a few days at least. So ask the seller about the contents of the hand-rearing food and ask for a sample. Also ask for him to be given a feed before you leave—not only to ensure that he goes home with a full crop but so that you can see the method used—either spoon or syringe. However, if he has been syringe-fed into the crop and you have not done this before, change to spoon-feeding. This is much safer for the inexperienced. A syringe can be a lethal instrument in

When your parrot is travelling by car in a pet carrier, place the seatbelt through the handle in the top of the carrier.

unskilled hands. A hungry bird will usually feed from a spoon even if he has not been used to this form of feeding. However, do be sure to clean any spilt food off the plumage immediately.

If he has had access to toys, ask the breeder or previous owner which kind he likes best. The preferences of individual birds vary greatly. It can save a lot of time and money to find out first!

If you are travelling home by car, on no account allow the bird to be loose inside the vehicle. Although it might seem very tame in its normal surroundings, in the strange environment of a car it will probably react quite differently. Unless you have a large vehicle, your bird's cage will not fit inside. Buy a plastic pet carrier, the type normally made for cats and dogs, and place the bird inside for the journey. If the back seat is empty, use the seat belt to secure the carrier, by passing the belt through the handle at the top.

When you arrive home, if your bird is tame he will probably step on to your hand and allow himself to be placed in his new cage. If he is not, open the door of the carrier and quickly place it against the open door of his cage. He will probably walk in but may need a little persuasion.

If your new pet is a small bird, such as a lovebird or cockatiel, and has been placed in a small box, on no account put your hand inside the box to remove him. He may be very nervous inside the dark box and is likely to bite in these circumstances. The correct method is to place the box inside the cage, open the box and allow him to come out when he is ready.

In your eagerness to please, do not fill his cage with toys or it will seem to be a very confusing place. One toy is enough at first. The others can be left near the cage so that he becomes familiar with the sight of them.

There is one mistake that many new parrot owners make. In their enthusiasm for the bird to be part of the family, they either allow him to spend long periods outside his cage or they permit him to come out at mealtimes and share their food. Don't do this! How many times has a new owner found that his parrot is reluctant to or actually refuses to feed from the food container in his cage? In desperation they telephone the seller who is quite mystified about this. What they have forgotten to mention is the fact that the parrot is allowed out at mealtimes. For parrots, eating is a social behaviour. They want to join in at family mealtimes. If allowed to do so during the early period in the new home, the young parrot will associate food with the table. He no longer wants to eat when he is inside his cage. The result can be that he rapidly loses weight. Either eat in a different room from your parrot or give him a small piece of nonfattening healthy food from your plate such as fruit, vegetables, bread, pasta, lean meat, yoghurt or cereal.

The other reason why he should not be allowed out at mealtimes is because when you have guests for dinner they will not appreciate a parrot walking across their dinner plates! And if you confine him to his cage, he will scream to be let out and make conversation impossible!

From the very first day, you must start as you intend to go on. Remember that if you teach your parrot bad habits from the beginning (they may seem amusing at first), it will be extremely difficult to break these habits when the joke has worn thin. Parrots are no different to children in that you have to teach them the acceptable way to behave.

On the subject of children, do not allow them to overwhelm with attention the new member of your family. And do not allow your bird to be passed round and handled like a toy, on that first day. Until he has settled in, it is best just to allow two adults to handle him. Make sure that during the early days your parrot has a quiet period free from distraction three times a day. This should help him to acquire routine feeding patterns. From the very first, place the cage in a carefully chosen location. This should not be the kitchen. Fumes from overheated nonstick pans have killed many birds. The birds will die within minutes. Often the owner is totally at a loss to know why. Cookers and sinks are dangerous places. Locate his cage in the most lived-in room in the house which is not the kitchen. Do not place the cage near a television set—as far away from it as possible is recommended. The eternal flashing lights from the screen are only acceptable for short periods. If the television is on all day, this room is not a good environment for a parrot, unless the room is large.

On that first day, make sure that your parrot goes to sleep with a full crop. There may be too many distractions for him to have eaten much on his own. If this is the case, a spoon-feed before bed will leave him contented.

Chapter 6

Living with a parrot

I often flinch when I watch how people who are unused to parrots behave when they are near them. Parrots respond well to those who are quiet and calm in their demeanour. When someone suddenly flings out their arm or makes jerky movements an aviary bird will fly to the furthest perch. A bird in a cage, unless hand-reared, may crouch in terror or even fall off its perch. Even very tame parrots react nervously. A parrot is designed to take flight at the first sign of danger, real or imagined. It does not wait to find out if its alarm is misplaced. If it did it would end up in the jaws or the talons of a predator. It therefore reacts instantly to something which makes it nervous. So many people are unaware that their behaviour is causing a bird stress.

Tell visitors that they must act with respect around your parrot.

Here are common ways in which stress is caused.
- Sudden or jerky movements, especially involving the arms and pointing.
- Standing too close to the cage or placing a finger inside the cage.
- Wearing a very bright, solid colour, especially bright red. Bright colours are more acceptable if broken up into patterns.
- Wearing a hat if the bird is not used to seeing someone with a hat.
- Wearing large gloves.
- Carrying a refuse sack, large bag or camera case, for example.
- Pointing at the cage using a stick or other long object.
- Cleaning above the cage with a long-handled brush.
- Allowing an unknown animal (dog or cat) to approach the cage.
- To a lesser degree, wearing glasses when this is not usual.
- Placing a large unfamiliar object close to the cage.
- Continual or loud arguing.

Parrots are very sensitive creatures who pick up good and bad "vibes" from people. I have seen them respond positively in seconds to people who love birds and know how to behave around them. I have also seen them respond negatively instantly to people who have kept birds for years and yet still do not understand what makes them fearful. So I will repeat: be calm, don't speak too loudly and above all don't throw your arms about. These guidelines should apply to everyone who comes into contact with your bird. This includes visitors. Before they even take their first step towards the cage, explain politely that your bird will be frightened by a close or noisy approach by someone he does not know.

Touching your parrot
In Chapter 1 it was explained that parrots can be divided into two groups, which I called Group A and Group B. Those in Group A are affectionate and the pair bond is strong. These birds spend hours in mutual preening, especially cockatoos. They therefore like to have their head scratched because this is the equivalent of preening. If you watch a pair of cockatoos preening each other they will preen everywhere, even under the other bird's wings. This means that when you are handling a tame cockatoo who is

bonded to you, you can do the same. Macaws and conures also preen each other over almost every part of the body.

Amazons usually only preen each other's head and neck; most Amazons do not like to be touched under the wings because this is not normal behaviour between a mated pair. In Group B birds, such as eclectus and ringnecks, if mutual preening occurs at all it is brief and usually confined only to the period of courtship. This means that most of these birds do not like to have the head scratched. They do not become "cuddly tame" like cockatoos and macaws. Therefore you must respect the natural behaviour of the species which shares your home. If you try to scratch his head against his will, he will try to get away or may even bite. When the bond between you and him is greater he may permit this liberty; on the other hand he may never do so. Don't expect every bird to enjoy being touched and held. Not all do, even those of Group A.

Mutual preening

A parrot in Group A (see Chapter 1) which is closely bonded to its owner will expect its head to be preened. Gentle fingers are just as good as a beak! Most parrots do not like areas other than the head to be scratched or tickled; cockatoos are an exception. However, individuals of all species vary in this and the owner must respect the bird's wishes. When a parrot is moulting the new feathers are encased in little waxy sheaths. A parrot cannot remove those on its head, which is one reason why mutual preening is so important in a pair of birds. His mate preens his head and he preens his mate. This helps to reinforce the pair bond. Parrots invite mutual preening by lowering the head slightly. If you see your parrot doing this, you will know he is inviting you to rub his head. In a close bond between parrot and owner the parrot may preen the owner's hair or facial skin. In the latter case they also like to remove tiny particles of salt. My Amazon sometimes "preens" around my eyes. This is the ultimate sign of affection which you will see only in a closely bonded pair of birds. It is a sign of trust, presumably because the eyes are so important and very vulnerable to rough preening. When your parrot is moulting, his head is quite tender; be extra careful when preening him and try to avoid the developing feathers. The waxy sheaths are fairly loose. On no account try to remove sheaths which are hard as this means the feathers are not fully formed and you will destroy them if you break the sheaths.

Discipline

It is very important that the new parrot owner knows how to react when his or her parrot is not behaving as one would hope. The reaction should always be the same and should be designed to deter this behaviour in a kind but firm manner. Only in this way will the parrot understand that that particular behaviour is not acceptable. If the reaction varies, the bird will become very confused.

If you have a young parrot, regard it like a child. It is vitally important that it receives discipline at an early age. If it does not, by the time it is six months old, like an undisciplined teenager, it will be out of control. In Chapter 12 basic training, such as teaching the bird to step on to your hand, is described.

Again, follow the behaviour of any good parent and don't shout, swear or smoke in the presence of your parrot. Shouting is loud and threatening and your swear words may be copied. Being in a smoke-filled environment is very harmful for a parrot. Inhalation of the smoke can result in chronic lung and air-sac conditions. Indeed, one top avian vet apparently refuses to treat pet birds whose owners smoke. He says it is a waste of time....

Establishing the bond

Loving care is so important. That love can only be mutual if your bird trusts you totally. That trust can be established only if you are calm and gentle. Never lose your temper, shout or handle him roughly. Return him to the cage immediately if he does something which he knows is wrong, such as nipping. Don't become annoyed if he bites a hole in your shirt or removes a button. Look him in the eyes, give a firm: "No!" and return him to the cage. Do the same next time. In this way you are establishing that this form of behaviour is not acceptable. You must take corrective action instantly or he will not know why you have acted as you have done.

"Prime time"

The time he spends out of the cage with you is prime time. He can sit with you while you watch television. Some parrots like to watch television for short periods. They can recognise birds and animals. My Amazon watches television with me for a short time every evening. She is interested in programmes, such as those on natural history, in which other birds appear. She will give an alarm call at the sight of a bird of prey or react with interest to another parrot. She also likes to look out of the window. In one house in which I lived, she would spend hours sitting on a large ornament (a cockatoo!) which was placed on a window sill, looking out of the window. This is acceptable only if a bird is not in strong sunlight and if it does no damage to window frame or wall.

Don't let a bird do such damage! Once it starts, it will believe that this is permissible behaviour and could soon wreck a room.

It is very important that parrots are not left in a room unsupervised. Not only can they come to harm (see Chapter 16) but

The time your parrot spends out of his cage, with your undivided attention, is "prime time."

if they cause damage the owner may be tempted to relegate them permanently to the cage. This would be highly regrettable because the bond between bird and owner is best reinforced by the two spending daily periods in physical contact.

Screaming

With the exception of greys, you can expect at least one daily period of screaming, if you keep one of the larger parrots. The smaller species can also be noisy but as the volume is lower this is less of a problem. If you are not prepared for some noise, you should not have chosen a parrot to be your companion. But continual shrieking for your attention is another matter. Unless you deal with the problem from the outset, it could spoil the pleasure which you would otherwise have in your parrot.

When your parrot yells or screams, what you must NOT do is to go running to the cage to tell him to be quiet. This is just the reaction he is looking for—getting you attention! Assuming that your bird has regular periods outside the cage every day, he is not neglected, therefore he should not be feeling insecure. Thus when he screams it is often just attention seeking. I have two ways of dealing with this. If I am not doing something in that room which demands my presence at that time, I tell the bird (my Amazon or my lory): "I can't stand this noise. Bye, bye!" and walk out of the room. As soon as I have left, she or he stops screaming. There is no point in continuing, since she or he can no longer attract my attention.

Alas, it is not always so simple if I need to be in that room. In that case I ignore the bird for a while, before deploying the distraction technique. This should be varied as much as possible so that the bird does not associate screaming with what it will perceive as a reward. This is because I then do something to occupy the bird's attention. I might get out the sprayer and spray them both. When I have finished they will be busy preening their plumage. Or, if the Amazon is screaming, I might go outside and pick them some sowthistle from the garden; that will keep her busy, eating the roots first. If it is in the morning and the cage has not yet been cleaned out, I will do that, because it will distract them. Or I might get the Amazon the cardboard centre from a roll of kitchen towel. If these tactics fail, I simply cover the cage.

If you can anticipate when your parrot will be noisy (some birds scream when you leave the room), try to keep him occupied just before you leave. Fold up a magazine and push it through the bars, give him a nut or a favourite toy which he has not seen for a while. The aim is to prevent screaming, when possible.

All this must be done with no fuss and without looking at the bird for longer than is necessary. Never, ever scream at a parrot to be quiet. It will love the drama and will yell even louder. And can you think of anything worse than a parrot which repeats "Shut up!"—or worse? It says a lot about the owner!

However, you need to understand what is making your parrot scream. It is not necessarily demanding attention. Many parrots yell in response to certain noises. These are most likely to be television, radio, music in any form, the vacuum cleaner or running water. If you keep other parrots, the sound of them calling from outside may be an invitation to return those calls. Therefore, the first thing to do when a parrot starts to scream is to lower the volume of sounds around it. Often, when I turn off the radio, my lory stops screaming immediately.

Listen to what he tells you

Many people expect parrots to talk to them in our language, so it is only fair that we should attempt to understand theirs. When you get to know a parrot well, you will begin to read his body language. You will also understand—if you are observant enough—that certain sounds have specific meanings. By listening to certain not very pronounced sounds which my Amazon makes, and without even looking at her, I know when she is "asking" for something which I am eating or preparing, or asking to be moved out of the sun, for example. I would emphasise that these are not human words but sounds which I had to learn. By being acquainted with the normal behaviour of a bird—and I do not mean only those in a pet situation—we can receive messages from them, in that we are alerted to some form of behaviour that is not usual.

The eye of a male Amazon, such as this blue-front, will always dilate when the bird is about to act aggressively.

For example, I have a breeding pair of parrots, the only pair in my collection which was wild-caught. They are not tame—in fact they are quite nervous. One day when I had finished feeding my birds, I noticed the male of the pair behaving strangely. He was craning his head backward and forwards in an attempt to catch my attention. When I went toward him I saw at once why. Instead of replacing his food dish, I had left it at the side. He had no food!

Courtship feeding and sexual maturity

In most, but not all, parrot species, the male feeds the female during the breeding season. Someone told me how he rushed his Amazon to the vet when it was apparently vomiting. In fact the Amazon was only trying to feed his owner! How can you distinguish the two actions? First, courtship feeding is often, but not always, preceded by elaborate head movements. Secondly, the very demeanour of the bird should tell you whether it is healthy and regurgitating or sick and vomiting. A parrot which is bright-eyed, alert and active is unlikely to be vomiting. A healthy parrot, especially a male, will want to demonstrate his affection during the breeding season by offering you his part-digested meal. Male or female, he or she may want to mate with your hand or arm. There is nothing wrong with this; it is just a way of releasing sexual energy. My female Amazon, for example, will crouch in my lap, shivering her wings, and making a continuous sound which is difficult to describe, but which is never heard at any other time. I can expect this to happen in May or June.

Aggressive encounters

These indications of breeding condition are not difficult to deal with. The real problem comes with the male Amazon or macaw or another species who chases people with intent to do harm. A parrot which has been disciplined with kindness from an early age is unlikely to do this; the problem is most likely to arise with a bird purchased as an adult. Its early history is unknown—and may have been a sad one. Situations do arise when people are chased by parrots, usually macaws, Amazons (especially excitable species like double yellow-heads, yellow-napes and blue-fronts) or pionus. They will try to attack a person's ankles or feet. The worst thing that someone in this situation can do is to run away, because the thrill of the chase will make the parrot extremely excited. If it is known that this is likely to occur, a large towel should be kept ready. The towel should be dropped over the bird who should be returned immediately to his cage. When the towel is covering the parrot, make sure you know where his beak is, and hold it through the towel on either side of the mandibles, so that he cannot bite. If you do not hold him correctly, he will bite you through the towel. This type of behaviour is most likely to occur if you allow your parrot to claim part of the house as his own territory. Be warned! If the pupils of his eyes contract to pin points, if he flares his tail and slightly opens his wings, all the while muttering and screaming excitedly, an attack is imminent. This is the worst time to try to handle him as, in his wild excitement, he will bite. He is defending his territory!

If a parrot is strongly bonded to one person, he could behave aggressively towards that person's partner. After all, it is normal for a male parrot to ward off competition during the breeding season. For the safety of everyone concerned, the bird should be confined to its cage or, better still, perhaps placed in an indoor or out-door flight where he can get some exercise. If this happens during summer, an outdoor flight with access to fresh air, sun and rain, will do him a world of good for a couple of months. However the flight should be close to the owner's house or he will feel that he has been abandoned. He should be visited several times daily with tid-bits.

Incidentally, while some parrot behaviourists will tell you that a pet should not be allowed to form a strong bond with one member of the household, that advice is hardly realistic. There are many circumstances in which such a bond is inevitable. Perhaps most common is when the parrot makes the choice and nothing will deter him or her from lavishing all its affection on one person.

The desire to breed

The desire to breed may be triggered by something which the parrot perceives as a desirable nest site. It could be a drawer which has been left open or the area behind floor-length curtains. The fact that the parrot does not have a mate of its own kind is irrelevant. If it sees a certain area as its nest, it will aggressively protect this area. This knowledge may help to overcome the problem.

It is perfectly natural for a mature bird to show some form of sexual behaviour. However, this does not necessarily mean that the bird needs a mate. In some cases this might be the case—if it has never responded to human companionship.

However, if the bird appears contented and has a close relationship with its owner, obtaining a mate could be an enormous mistake. One cannot generalise on this point and it is very difficult for anyone who does not know the birds to give advice. The point to bear in mind is that the owner should not automatically feel guilty that his or her parrot does not have a mate. Obtaining a bird of the opposite sex could be a total disaster for all concerned or it could be the introduction of a successful breeding pair. The outcome can never be predicted.

It is fair to issue a warning, however. Pairing up your pet bird is potentially disastrous. I will relate what happened when I unwisely gave my yellow-fronted Amazon a mate. Although the

54

male was very interested in her, she ignored him completely. As far as she was concerned, I was her mate. However, the nest-box delighted her and stimulated her to lay. This act nearly killed her. I saw with horror that she had a prolapse of the oviduct. Left untreated, this is fatal. I rushed her to the nearest vet who made a purse-string suture of the vent. In other words, he tied up the cloaca so that she could defecate but in a way which prevented another prolapse. She made a full recovery and I never again allowed her near a nest-box or a male. Why did she have a pro-lapse? As a pet bird, she simply was not breeding fit and was slightly overweight. This is a very important point to consider as overweight females are very susceptible to a prolapse or to egg-binding. If a pet bird is rehomed for breeding purposes, it should be allowed to fly in a flight to become really fit before it is intro-duced to its potential mate. This applies with male or female.

Alone in the house
If you must go out for long periods, leaving your parrot totally alone, it is a good idea to leave the radio playing. Turn it to a music station, as music is the most stimulating sound. You will soon discover which kind of music your bird prefers. Amazons love vocal music, especially opera, and many will try to sing-along. This really keeps them happy! If you will only be out for half an hour, leave a cassette tape playing. Before you go out, close the blinds if necessary, so that the cage will not be in direct sunlight.

Covering the cage at night
Is this necessary? It depends on the location of the cage. If your parrot lives in a room where there is much human activity and/or television after 9 P.M., the answer is: yes. The cage should also be covered if street lights or lights from passing traffic enter the room. A cover of fairly heavy dark material should be made to fit right over the cage. It should be removed early in the morning.

Is one parrot enough?
It happens so often! Delighted with the first parrot, the owner or owners decide that they would like another one, usually a totally different species. They fail to realise that their bird will be

extremely jealous. It has been the centre of attention; another parrot is competition for that attention. So often, it results in the relationship between parrot and owner being totally altered. Parrots are so demanding of attention and affection that few people can take on a second bird without jeopardising their relationship with the first. It is rather like taking on a lover when you are married. One relationship will not survive! A second bird might be a success in a family, where different people are responsible for each bird.

Going on a journey

The time will come when you need to take your parrot on a journey, perhaps to the vet, or even on holiday with you. For a journey to the vet the use of a plastic pet carrier or a stronger type of pet carrier, as made for dogs and cats, is recommended. If the species is a small one, take him in his own cage, assuming that you are travelling by car. This sometimes helps to provide a clue to the problem, as the vet can see how the bird is kept. If you are transporting a small bird and you have to walk, a small strong box may be better. If your bird accompanies you on holiday, either a plastic pet carrier or a small cage which will fit into the vehicle can be used. Make sure that you have one or the other at hand; you never know when you might need it. Remember, of course, that if you live in the U.K., you cannot take your bird overseas on holiday because he would have to be quarantined for 35 days on your return! Also, many charter airlines do not have a licence to carry livestock.

When you go on holiday

When you go away, who will look after your parrot? This is something which MUST be considered before you become a parrot owner. If there are several people in your household, one of whom can take care of him, this is the ideal solution. But do be certain that they know exactly how he is fed and his preferences. A parrot should not be left alone for more than one day. Somebody coming in on a daily basis to give him food and water is not acceptable. He will be lonely and miserable and may resort to plucking his feathers. If you can find someone to take him into his home, this may be a good idea provided that:

- Your bird already knows this person.

- He or she does not have any birds of their own. The disease risk is too great!

If the carer does know your bird, it is a good idea that your parrot should spend a day with him or her before you go away. If some problem arises, possibly due to the lack of knowledge of something quite simple, you can advise. Some parrots refuse to eat during their first day in strange surroundings. You can be prepared for this by having ready some favourite food items. Always leave written instructions about everything you can think of.

If you live alone

If you live alone, what would happen to your parrot if, for example, you were suddenly taken into hospital? Think about this carefully and make an arrangement with a trustworthy friend. Give written instructions at the time and leave a copy in your house, preferably in your telephone book. This is probably the first place someone would look if they were trying to contact a relative. Also make sure that you leave instructions regarding your parrot in your will. If you fail to do so, he may end up at an auction or in a pet store.

An unwanted parrot

If your circumstances change and you can no longer keep your parrot, or if you know that he would have a better life with someone who can devote more time to him, what should you do? Unless you know a suitable person who can take him, I believe that the best solution is to advertise him in one of the magazines listed on page 128 and 150. What you should not do is to give him away, unless it is to a close friend or trusted person. In this · case make a stipulation that if this person cannot keep him, he returns him to you. If you give him away, the temptation to sell him for a quick profit may be great. If you advertise your bird, the price must be exactly right. Most people are looking for a young bird so you may not attract any buyers if the price is too high. Be aware that if it is too low, you will attract dealers. Ask prospective purchasers any questions you believe are necessary to establish if your parrot will go to a good home and do not feel you must sell to the first one who responds. Tell them you will call them back.

What should you do if your bird is plucked or is unsaleable for some other reason? This is a difficult question to answer. Perhaps the best suggestion is to advertise him with complete honesty at a low price, explaining why the price is low. There are some caring people who cannot afford to pay the full price and who will persevere with a bird which no-one else wants. There are also parrot rescue centres. Some are run by genuine people. Others masquerade under the name to obtain parrots for nothing which they can sell on. Before contacting such a place, try to make independent enquiries about it and ask if you can visit the centre.

Chapter 7

Weaning the purchased pet

First of all, I must state that I am totally against the sale of unweaned parrots. There should be a law against it. Every year many young parrots die within weeks of going to a new home. This is either due to the inexperience of the buyer or because the seller has told the buyer that the parrot is weaned when, in fact, this is far from the truth. I refer especially to the larger parrots such as large macaws and cockatoos. Some breeders truly believe that such birds can be weaned at 14 weeks and they sell them at this age. This is what I would describe as forced weaning. The smaller parrots such as greys and Amazons are normally weaned by this age and this is the best time for them to go to a new home. Large macaws and cockatoos are not totally weaned until the age of about five months, possibly not until six months. Those which are force-weaned at an early age will be whining and begging for food, anxious and hungry. Their growth may be stunted. It will be more difficult for them to adjust during the stressful period of moving to a totally different environment. This will evince itself as a reluctance to feed and constant crying or begging to come out of the cage, for attention and reassurance. Of course all young birds want to come out, but the well adjusted, properly weaned one will appear happy and playful and will spend long periods eating, even if he does still want a spoon-feed every day.

Before buying a large parrot the hatch date should be established. A reputable breeder should have no objection to showing you his or her records. If no records are kept, you can doubt the efficiency of other areas of husbandry. All serious breeders keep records.

The behaviour of a young parrot when it reaches its new home is partly dependent on how it has been hand-reared. The best hand-rearers place great emphasis on psychological welfare. One of these is Phoebe Greene Linden from California. She wrote (Linden, 1996): "The pervasive theme of all socialisation is, in my mind, teaching young birds how to trust. We want them to trust that their surroundings are safe and interesting. We introduce toys and encourage the chicks to play soon after their eyes open. Additionally, we want the birds to trust in profuse food supply. Moreover, trust regarding people must extend beyond the primary handfeeder to include other humans who are loving and solicitous. A firm foundation of trust allows chicks to thrive on psychological, mental and physical levels."

This underlines that weaning is more than teaching a young parrot to become independent where food is concerned. If several young parrots are reared together they will spend much time playing and interacting with each other but they still need the attention of the person or persons who fed them. This attention should not cease suddenly or the young ones will feel insecure and less likely to want to eat on their own. This is especially so with a young parrot which has been reared on its own. The handfeeder is the centre of its world. It is likely to take longer to wean than those reared with companions. If possible, it should be placed next to another parrot of about the same size (species immaterial). The companionship and the opportunity to watch another bird feeding will assist its development. Eating is a social activity; one of the reasons why single parrots are slower to wean is because they lack the incentive to eat which is stimulated in a group of birds.

A friend who has hand-reared more than 100 greys, usually a minimum of two or three at a time, never had any problems weaning them. They normally went to their new homes at the age of about 14 weeks. Then came a single chick, a female. She was not totally weaned until the age of six months. As she was perfectly healthy, this can be attributed to the fact that she had been reared on her own. Throughout the period, she was kept in the breeder's house and treated as one of the family, as she still is today.

Love and affection are vital for the well-being of a young parrot in a new home.

Now let us consider further the task of taking on a 14-week-old cockatoo or macaw. This might be acceptable provided that the person is not new to hand-feeding and that the bird is still on two feeds, perhaps even three, per day. The new owner must realise that weaning is a VERY gradual process. A few exceptional breeders of the large macaws allow the young to stay with their parents until they are nine to 12 months old. In the wild, young macaws would spend about one year with their parents. Is it any wonder that there are problems when forced weaning is carried out when they are little more than three months old? This is acceptable for the galah (roseate or rose-breasted cockatoo) and for the bare-eyed cockatoo (little Corella) because they have a shorter fledging time (and a shorter incubation period). Moluccan and umbrella cockatoos will react badly to early weaning. They will be psychologically and physically stunted. When I hand-reared Moluccan cockatoos at Palmitos Park, many people commented on their large size. This was because I did not wean them until the age of five or six months. On one occasion, when I was on holiday, two Moluccans were weaned at just over four months of age. They never quite attained the size of the other young from the same two pairs. Many people find that Moluccan cockatoos are among the hardest parrots to wean. This is because they try to wean them too early. The result is that they continually whine to be fed, even at the age of nine months—possibly

61

longer. They have spent so much of their young lives in a state of hunger and anxiety that whining becomes a habit.

Here is a piece of information of use to the breeder, rather than to the pet owner—information which will permit breeders to rear young which will make better pets. I completely eliminated crying in young Moluccan cockatoos.

When they were nearly fully feathered but still on about five feeds a day, at about six or seven weeks, I would isolate them with an adult male. At first he was placed in an adjoining cage. As soon as the young ones were old enough to fly, all would be released together in an indoor enclosure of which they were the only occupants. The young cockatoos never whined to be fed. I visited them five times a day and they enjoyed my company but did not show the clinging behaviour typical of Moluccans reared without the presence of an adult of their own species.

Young parrots that are force-weaned are often desperate for attention. They must feel so insecure. In order to obtain attention they develop undesirable habits such as screaming or throwing down their food pots. One lady who consulted me had an 11-month-old umbrella cockatoo which was still on one feed a day and not eating well on its own. Its constant screaming, which abated only when it was let out of its cage, and its habit of throwing down the food dishes (up to 14 times a day) led to her parting with it at 11 months. Unfortunately, she had been given very poor advice on its weaning from every source she had consulted. It seemed unlikely that any of these people had ever weaned a cockatoo themselves.

So, what are the key factors in successful weaning. There are two: 1) the process should be gradual and the pace should be dictated by the individual bird; 2) the bird should never be allowed to become very hungry.

Weaning age

The personalities of young parrots become evident at an early age. Parrots are individuals. It is impossible to say that, for example, a blue-fronted Amazon must be weaned by 12 weeks. There are no rules relating to species and age at weaning.

There is one general rule that should always be adhered to: young birds should never be allowed to become excessively hungry. The most common mistake is to reduce the number of feeds too soon. Many feeders do this in order to reduce their work load. A hungry chick is an unhappy one that begs for food and does not want to feed itself. Instead of reducing the number of feeds, the best action is to reduce the amount of food being given at each feed. Do not completely fill the crop. After being fed, the young parrot will start nibbling at some of the items offered. In other words, feeding him (not overfeeding) stimulates him to finish off his meal by himself.

Only when he is spending a lot of time each day nibbling at food, some of which is consumed, can one reduce the number of feeds. When you take him out for a feed, feel the crop (the area situated below the throat). If he is reluctant to feed from the spoon and there is solid food in the crop (rather than the more liquid hand-fed food), it is time to cut out a feed. However, reluctance to feed could have another cause. This is especially the case with large macaws. When first removed from the cage they have a great need to flap their wings. Many refuse to feed until they have done so. As they approach weaning age, some parrots refuse the first feed of the day. This does not matter. But it is important that they have a full crop at night.

To demonstrate a very general guide, I will show the feeding schedule for three red-bellied parrots (*Poicephalus rufiventris*), which I had to remove from the nest at the age of four weeks. This species normally spends 11 weeks in the nest.

Age	Number of daily feeds
Four weeks	6
Six weeks	5—nibbling at food
Eight weeks	4—first flight
Eight and a half weeks	3
Ten and a half weeks	2
Eleven and a half weeks	1
Twelve and a half weeks	Independent

Red-bellied parrots hand-reared by the author.

Weaning is, of course, accompanied by a loss of weight. In the nest a parent-fed bird has reached adult weight before it fledges. It needs to lose some of this weight in order to be able to fly well. Therefore, just before fledging, a slight loss of appetite is natural. Except in cockatoos, in which the breast bone may be a little prominent, the young parrot should not appear to be thin. If it is, it is either suffering from malnutrition, has worms or is sick. An avian vet should be consulted.

There are many different views on weaning parrots, some of them conflicting and some offered by those who are not qualified to do so. If advice is needed, consult the breeder, if known. However, some breeders (especially in the U.S.A.) sell all their young before they are weaned and may have no experience whatsoever of weaning parrots. In this case, seek advice from someone who has extensive experience of hand-rearing AND weaning. Vets are not necessarily a good source of information on this subject, unless they have personal experience, but they may know a breeder who can help.

As I previously stated, parrots are individuals and rules do not apply. But it is useful to have a guide to weaning ages, which differ according to the species. The expected weaning age can be calculated approximately by taking the age at which the species would leave the nest, if parent-reared, and adding on two or three weeks for the medium-sized parrots, such as greys and Amazons, and about ten days for small species, such as lovebirds. As a general guide, Amazons wean at ten to 12 weeks and greys and eclectus at about 14 weeks. As already mentioned, the larger parrots take much longer. The slowest to wean are the black cockatoos (*Calyptorhynchus*), such as the red-tailed black, which takes nine months or more. The quickest parrots to wean are lories and lorikeets. They will usually lap a warm liquid food before they are even fully feathered. Initially this can be the food on which they were reared. When they are feeding themselves well, this can be mixed with the liquid food (a commercial lory food made up from powder) which will be the basis of the adult diet. The usual fruits and vegetables should also be offered.

Weaning foods

Different parrot species have different dietary needs, thus the foods offered at weaning depend on the species. However, it is important to offer a variety of items.

Food-wise, parrots are at their most adventurous when they are young. If they are encouraged to eat many different items at this age, the habit should stay with them throughout their lives. A dietary deficiency is more likely in birds which accept very few items, unless pellets are included, as these are manufactured as a complete diet. Nevertheless, no bird (or human) should live on 100 percent processed foods. Fruits, vegetables, green leaves and cereals provide variety in taste, colour and texture.

Colour is important to parrots. Young birds are attracted by green, red and orange; pieces of orange or apple, raw carrot, fresh corn and green beans are always examined and nibbled with interest. Soft wholegrain bread, crackers and wholemeal biscuits are also enjoyed. Species large and small like spray millet, especially eclectus and cockatoos. The smaller parakeets and lovebirds can be offered spray millet, bread and leaves of spinach beet. Gradually, as they consume, rather than play with, these items, their normal diet can be introduced. At this stage they should be familiarised with extruded pellets and with seeds and, in the case of the larger species, cooked foods such as maize and beans. The two dietary bases to which fresh fruits and vegetables are added are pellets and seeds. Learning about both types of foods is an advantage. It helps to ensure that if the parrot is suddenly rehomed it will at least be familiar with the food offered.

Phoebe Linden described another type of weaning food which is excellent in every respect. As soon as chicks show an interest in manipulating food, cooked warm foods (at a temperature of 43°C or 110°F) are offered. She recorded: "Even at this early age, we serve, hot and wet: whole wheat toast strips soaked in juice; cooked pasta; baked potato and squash [courgettes]; mango, papaya, banana and more.... The eager young enjoy being fed from the hand."

She has found that this feeding technique teaches even the novice hand-feeder a new basic skill and enhances interaction as well as nutrition. Under supervision, several young people participate in the feeding process, thus teaching the young parrots to socialise with humans. This helps to prepare them for their new home. Phoebe Linden also uses food as toys, by tying with rawhide strips bunches of greens such as spinach and chard, in the box in which the young are kept. In this way young parrots combine food and toys as integral components of development.

Transition feeding

When a young parrot goes to a new home, everything which was safe and familiar in its life is removed: the feeders, the other young ones with whom it was reared, the cage and the environment. It may be too nervous to eat. Even if a young parrot is sold to you as fully weaned, it will almost certainly need to be spoon-fed, or syringe-fed, for at least three days. Only if it is well fed will it feel secure and start to relax. Then it will eat on its own. Spoon-feeding will also help to forge the bond with its new owner.

Never forget that eating is a social behaviour. A single parrot kept in a room where the family eats will often go down to the food dish and start to eat at family mealtimes. You may need to teach a young parrot how to eat certain foods. A good way to do this is by example. Perhaps you have him out each evening when you are watching television. Put the food you wish him to eat on a plate and eat it, or pretend to eat it, yourself. It is amazing how desirable a food item suddenly becomes if the bird believes it is not intended for him!

Chapter 8

Food for pleasure and health

Any vet who sees a substantial number of pet parrots in his practice will tell you the same thing: most of them are brought in suffering from dietary deficiencies which have caused a wide variety of illnesses. Probably diseases related to the lack of Vitamin A are the most common. In grey parrots this would be closely followed by problems arising from a calcium deficiency. In budgerigars, goitre, due to an iodine deficiency, is common; so are tumours. Some species are more susceptible to certain problems. This is mainly diet-related.

It is a fact, sometimes overlooked by the beginner, that different species have different dietary needs. It is also true that aviary birds have different requirements to pet birds, in a temperate climate. In cold weather, birds in unheated aviaries need fats and oils as a source of energy. As pet birds live at room temperature and as they are less active (and many are not permitted to fly), they have a much lower requirement for fats and oils. For example, in winter, Amazon parrots kept in outdoor aviaries could consume quite a lot of sunflower seed; the same quantity given to a pet bird would result in it becoming grossly overweight. Therefore, before recommending a diet for a certain species, its circumstances also need to be considered. As this relates to companion birds, I would classify members of the parrot family into three broad groups:

1. Lories and lorikeets, the nectar-feeding specialists.
2. Other parrots, which need a low-fat diet.
3. Other parrots, which need a high-fat diet.

Group 1. The species most likely to be kept as pets are green-naped lorikeets (*Trichoglossus h. haematodus*), dusky lories (*Pseudeos fuscata*) and perhaps one of the larger *Lorius* species such as the yellow-backed (*L. garrulus flavopalliatus*) or the black-capped (*L. lory*). Some of the other lory species, which are seldom kept as pets, require nectar as about 85 percent of their diet. The frequently kept ones need at least 50 percent nectar in the diet. There are nectar mixes available, to which one adds only water. These are specially formulated for lories and are a virtually complete diet. Good examples are Lory Life by Avico in the U.S.A. and Nekton-Lori made by Nekton and available in Europe and the U.S.A. Most pet shops do not stock them. Stockists can be found by consulting avicultural magazines or contacting a lory breeder. It is not advisable to try to make up a nectar mixture, except in an emergency, as it will not be a properly balanced food. It might appear cheaper to do so, but as the bird will need to drink more to obtain all the necessary nutrients, it is not cheaper in actual fact. In addition, lories and lorikeets need fresh fruits and vegetables daily. Some may also eat cooked beans and cooked maize and a little sunflower seed, soaked or dry. Cranberry juice is beneficial and a little can be given on a regular basis.

Group 2. The birds in this group will soon become overweight and unhealthy if fed a diet with a high fat content. In other words, limit the sunflower seed. Roseate cockatoos (galahs) soon develop fatty tumours if fed on sunflower; they should be converted to a pelleted diet as soon as possible. Amazon and *Pionus* parrots will not live a long life on a diet which consists mainly of a parrot mixture. While this fact is well known, some owners

A good parrot and parrakeet mixture contains a variety of items. This one includes sunflower, saf-flower, pine nuts, oats, paddy rice, extruded pellets, broken maize, melon seeds and chillis (dried red peppers).

make little effort to vary the diet, claiming that their birds will not eat other items. Other owners simply cannot be bothered. This is very sad. All too often I hear of the death of a *Pionus* parrot, usually a much-loved pet, at an early age. Deaths are commonly due to respiratory problems. These are often induced by a deficiency of Vitamin A. One often sees Amazon parrots which are overweight, due to a lack of exercise and a poor diet. Many of these birds will die from kidney and/or liver problems. This is regrettable as it is not normally difficult to persuade Amazons to take a varied diet. Amazons and *Pionus* need a lot of fresh fruit, greenfood and vegetables, plus other items which I will term "human food." They can also be given beans, such as butter, haricot and chick peas (garbanzos) which have been soaked overnight, then boiled for about 15 minutes. The same applies to maize. Although other types of beans are often recommended, in my experience parrots only eat them if they have no choice.

Seed should not form more than 50 percent of the diet for this group. Seed must be offered fresh daily. The container should never be topped up; if this is done it will gradually contain more and more debris and husks until the bird has almost nothing to eat. In any case, the container must be washed daily. A mixture of seed should be provided in a small container; most parrots will simply discard or ignore the less favoured seeds if these are offered in a large one. Not only is this wasteful and expensive, it means that the bird can feast on its favourite seed only. Most owners of pet parrots automatically fill the food cup with seed, thereby discouraging their bird to sample other foods. If they can fill up on seed, the more reluctant eaters of fruit and vegetables will be less inclined to do so. There should be at least three containers in the cage: one for seed or pellets, one for fruits and vegetables, and one for water. Those who feed pellets may want to place fresh foods in the same container. This is acceptable; however, fruits and seeds may end up as a sticky mess.

Another reason for not permitting a bird to take sunflower seed as a large part of the diet is because of its variable quality, now that the best quality sunflower is often taken for human use. Test every batch of new seed by opening the kernels to examine the size of the kernel in relation to the husk; it should fill the husk, and the seed should be fairly plump, unless it is a small variety. Also taste it. A germination test can be made by soaking a small quantity of seed, then leaving it in a warm place to sprout. At least 70 percent of the seed should germinate. If it does not, return it to the supplier. If necessary, buy elsewhere. To help vary the content of a seed mixture, safflower seed can be used to replace about one third of the sunflower. Safflower is a small white seed. Pine nuts, the large Russian kind (dark brown), are favoured by many of the larger parrots. However, they have a fat content which is approximately the same as that of sunflower.

Group 3. The birds in this group have a need for a diet which is quite high in fats. Overweight birds are seldom seen. This is because in the wild they feed on the fruits (nuts) of palm trees. These fruits are oozing in oil. Birds in this group include Hyacinthine and other large macaws, and grey parrots. The macaws can be fed ad-lib nuts, such as Brazil and walnut, which are very high in fat. Greys can also be given these nuts—but not so many that they lose interest in other items.

Kashmir Csaky, a hyacinthine macaw specialist, questioned pet owners over a period of two and a half years regarding the cause of death of approximately 30 of these birds—the most expensive parrot one can own as a pet. Three died in accidents, five died from infectious diseases and the rest died from visceral gout. They had kidney and liver damage induced by a diet too rich in vitamin D3, according to Csaky (1997). It was not stated whether all of these birds had postmortem examinations, so the figures may not be quite accurate. Nevertheless, it underlines the major cause of death. The tragedy is that as this species has been available as a pet for a comparatively short time, probably most would have been young birds. When one considers how expensive it is to purchase a hyacinthine macaw, the deaths represent a huge financial loss as well as an emotional one which might deter the owner from ever again keeping another parrot. These losses also represent the deaths of birds of an endangered species; one might question whether they should be kept as pets, anyway.

The larger parrots love to hold a nut in the foot and remove the contents. This gives much more enjoyment than providing kernels only.

Kashmir Csaky commented: "A Hyacinth's diet should be high in fat and carbohydrates. Half of the diet should be composed of nuts and the majority of the nuts should be macadamia nuts in the shell." (These nuts are easily obtainable in the U.S.A. but not in Europe.)

The first decision to be made by the new parrot owner is whether his bird will be offered a diet based on seed or on pellets. Seed is deficient in a number of important nutrients, thus if it forms, say, 60 percent of the diet, the owner must ensure that the parrot consumes a variety of other items. This can be difficult with some species, if they have not been taught to eat various foods from the time they were weaned. A vitamin and mineral supplement will also be necessary.

When buying for one or two pet birds, it is advisable to buy seed in a packet from an established company. Loose seed from a small pet shop may be stale, a poor quality mix or even contaminated by mouse droppings. If the owner of a pet bird has other parrots, seed can be bought in quantity from importers who offer well-cleaned seed. Some parrot mixtures on the market consist of 90 percent sunflower seed. A quality mixture containing a wide variety of items is recommended.

Avoid peanuts unless the mixture is an expensive one. Some mixtures contain low-grade peanuts which can poison birds. I don't recommend feeding peanuts because of the risk; if peanuts are fed, buy those for human consumption from a health food store.

Nuts

Nuts are an extremely important part of the diet of the large macaws, especially the Hyacinthine. Suitable kinds are walnuts, almonds, Brazil nuts, macadamia, pecans and hazelnuts. They have a high fat content but do not contain significant quantities of saturated fat which might cause a problem in inactive birds. Only coconut is high in saturated fat. Brazil nuts are a good source of calcium and phosphorus, and almonds and hazelnuts also have a high calcium content. Parrots with a strong beak should be given whole nuts; they greatly enjoy opening them, also breaking up the shells. Some parrots will keep a piece of shell in the beak for long periods, grinding it and turning it round and round. Nuts offer more than nutrition; they provide beak exercise and amusement and keep the cutting edges of the beak in good repair. Whole nuts should not be rationed for the large macaws: offer as many as possible. For other species bear in mind the high fat content; the protein content is also high. According to Abramson et al (1995) total fat content is as follows: pecan 77 percent, macadamia 74 percent, Brazil 66 percent, hazelnut 63 percent, walnut 62 percent, black walnut 56 percent, almond 52 percent and coconut 33 percent. In the same analysis sunflower was 49.5 percent—although there would be a slight variation in fat content according to the variety of sunflower.

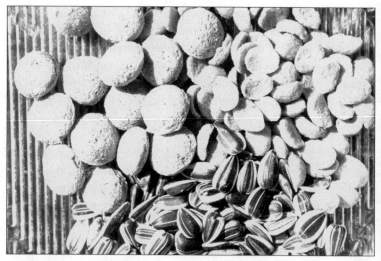

Large, striped sunflower seed contrasted with two types of pelleted foods: top left, malt parrot pellets by The Birdcare Company, U.K., and right, NutriBird P15 by Versele-Laga. Belgium (available in the U.K.).

Pellets

In the U.S.A., processed foods such as pellets and extruded foods for parrots have been available for some time. In Europe, parrot owners have been slower to embrace this new way of feeding. There is a tendency to refer to pellets and extruded foods as pellets—but they are not quite the same. Both contain such items as corn, wheat, oats, eggs, vitamins, minerals and amino acids, which are made into a mash. The extrusion or cooking process makes the food more palatable and easily digested. Extruded foods are cooked at very high temperatures; pellets are manufactured at lower temperatures.

Initially, palatability of pellets was poor; however, an increasing number of types are now available, and this aspect has received more attention. Given the choice, there are very few parrots who would choose pellets if they could eat sunflower. It is not a food which is attractive to many parrots. However, when pellets are fed as the basis of the diet, a dietary deficiency is unlikely. When seed is fed to the exclusion of other foods, a dietary deficiency is inevitable. It is seldom easy to convert birds from seed to pelleted diets; some birds refuse to be converted. They will die—and unfortunately have died — rather than eat pellets. Some simply do not recognise them as food. This is especially true of species which are naturally seed eaters, like Budgerigars. In fact, they can be kept in good condition on a diet of seed, greenfoods such as seeding grasses and chickweed, and a vitamin and mineral supplement. To try to force them on to a pelleted diet is ill-advised, in my opinion.

Inappropriate diets

Great care must be taken in trying to convert birds to a new diet. In 1996 a reader wrote to a well-known bird magazine regarding the diet of his or her cockatiel, which would eat only budgerigar mixture and millet spray. He refused dried and fresh fruits, vegetables and peanuts. On several occasions the owner tried to starve him into submission. He or she wrote: "A few times I have refused to fill his seed cup, thinking that when he got hungry enough, he would eat. After three or four days, I gave in."

73

First of all, I am appalled that anyone would treat a bird in such a callous manner. Secondly, I am surprised that he did not die before four days. After 48 hours without food, most smaller species such as the cockatiel, would be in a very bad condition. Thirdly, it is misguided to try to make a cockatiel eat a diet that is suited to a species with a totally different lifestyle. In the wild, cockatiels inhabit areas which are dry for perhaps eleven months of the year. They do not come from rainforests where there are fruits available year round. Their diet consists mainly of seeds. Peanuts and dried and fresh fruits are foreign to cockatiels, except some small berries. Captive-bred birds can exist for two or three decades on a diet consisting of seed, a slice of apple with a little vitamin and mineral supplement added to it, and fresh greenfoods such as chickweed, young dandelion leaves, sowthistle and spinach beet.

The larger parrots are a different matter. So many die from diet-related causes that a diet consisting of pellets, fruit and vegetables is good. Some manufacturers of pellets claim that their foods are a complete diet and the birds need nothing else.

They are considering diet only from the nutritionist's viewpoint. Everyone who keeps parrots knows that they enjoy their food just as much as we do. They revel in a variety of colours, tastes and textures. They are not chickens, with a minimal number of taste buds. To suggest that pellets are a complete diet is inhumane, in my opinion. One might also question the advisability of keeping a parrot on a 100 percent processed diet. Of course to some people pellets are wonderful news, as they are simply too lazy to go to any trouble to provide a varied diet. There is another point to consider. No one yet knows the long-term effects of feeding parrots on extruded pellets. The pellets have not been available long enough. My Amazon has been with me for over 30 years on a seed-based diet. Years ago, before the importance of Vitamin A was realised, she did suffer catarrh-like symptoms, which were almost certainly the result of a Vitamin A deficiency. These days she has half of a normal-sized food cup (capacity 50 g of, for example, sunflower seed) of seed, about 60 percent sunflower. The rest of her food consists of fresh fruits and vegetables and "human food" — cooked vegetables, cooked chicken, cooked fish, pasta, cereal, light crispbread, a small piece of fruit cake or cheese. When available, I give her chickweed and sowthistle from the garden, and hawthorn berries. Every morning she takes a little yoghurt from a spoon; a multivitamin mixture had been added to her yoghurt. I have offered her pellets, but I would not force them on her.

Pellets and fat requirement

My advice to anyone who buys a young parrot which has been weaned on to pellets would be to keep him on that food as the basis of the diet, plus fruits and vegetables. However, the owner must be certain that the pellets are of the correct kind for the species concerned. As mentioned above, the fat requirements vary. Some companies make pellets which take this into account. They name the species or group of parrots for which the various pellets are suitable. The best choice, in my opinion, is a company which produces pellets for a range of parrot species.

"Human foods"

Many items are suitable, such as those mentioned above. In addition, wholemeal bread and toast are enjoyed, and pizza and pasta. Only small amounts should be offered. Lean meat and well-cooked bones are excellent. Chop bones and part of the carcass of a chicken or turkey are a wonderful treat for cockatoos, macaws, eclectus, Amazons and even for smaller parrots. They provide protein, calcium, beak exercise and amusement. Avoid avocado, chocolate and items with a high sugar content. Do not let your bird drink alcohol or any drink except water and fruit juices.

Fruits

Fruits are valuable to provide fibre, vitamins, easily held objects, juice and colour, as well as a range of pleasant flavours. In most cases their food value is low—but this is no reason to withhold them. All fruits should be washed or peeled before feeding, because of the risk of contamination by pesticides. The most commonly fed are listed. Apple: golden delicious is favoured by many parrots. Pear: conference is a good type; do not feed hard. Grapes: some species eat them for the flesh while others only extract the

Fruits and vegetables popular with parrots are grapes, oranges and apple, corn on the cob, carrot and green beans. The peach is a stand-in for the popular pomegranate which was not available at the time!

pips. It is hardly worth feeding them to the latter. Banana: probably the most nutritious food we can offer. It is usually preferred in a medium-ripe condition. Offer a circular slice, in the skin, so that it can be held in the foot. Many parrots will ignore it without the skin. Oranges, satsumas and tangerines: relished by nearly all parrots; cut into pieces with the skin retained. The bird can then hold a piece in the foot without getting too much juice over the feet. These fruits must be sweet. If they are bitter they are usually ignored. However, some parrots will eat grapefruit! Pomegranate: the number one favourite of nearly all parrots. Unfortunately, the season is not long. As well as being popular, it contains high levels of Vitamin B2, Vitamin C and the mineral manganese. It should be offered when the skin (and therefore the contents) are ruby red. Those fortunate enough to live in a climate where pomegranates grow, should plant a tree, also guavas, another popular choice.

A variety of other, more exotic fruits, is also enjoyed, such as cactus fruits, loquats and lychees. There is no limit if the budget is also limitless! I have never had much success in trying to persuade parrots to take soft fruits such as strawberries, raspberries and gooseberries; plums, peaches and kiwi fruit are not too popular. Cherries are relished and species with strong beaks will open the stones. Peach stones are greatly enjoyed by the larger parrots who can open them and extract the kernel. The less popular fruits are worth offering on at least one occasion, as a few birds will eat them.

Finally, a mention of fruit stone kernels and pips, such as those from apples. I have seen it written that these are poisonous. This is not the case—although possibly they might be if they formed 100 percent of the diet!

Vegetables

In my experience, raw carrots and green beans are the most popular. Carrot may be ignored unless offered in an appropriate manner. Although it can be diced and added to a mixture, many birds prefer it when cut at an angle into pieces 7.5 cm to 10 cm (3 in. to 4 in.) long and wedged in the bars of the cage. Carrot and tomato are two of the most valuable foods that can be offered, due to their high Vitamin A content. Other foods in this beneficial category are the leaves of broccoli, kale and turnip. (Those who live in countries where yams are grown should note that they, too, have a high Vitamin A content, also high calcium content.) Red peppers and courgettes (squash) are also readily eaten, as is cooked beetroot. Small sticks of celery are a great favourite with some birds. Peas in the pod are very popular. Frozen peas which have been thawed can be substituted out of season—but buy a good brand. Warnings have been published about the sodium content of frozen vegetables. In fact there is normally only a trace—most pellets contain more. Many parrots like boiled potato while it is still warm. Chips should not be given to most parrots because of their high fat content. Fresh corn cut into small pieces is a universal favourite. Out of season tinned or frozen (thawed but not cooked) corn kernels are also relished. It should be noted that corn, banana and grapes should not be fed in large quantities because of the inverse ratio of phosphorus to calcium.

One could also offer freeze-dried fruits and vegetables. Many parrots enjoy dried banana and dried pineapple.

Growing your own greenfoods

Anyone can grow greenfoods for parrots; if you don't have a garden, a window box will do! If you don't have a window box grow cress from seed in little containers for smaller species! In the warmer months I pick chickweed and sowthistle from my garden; these weeds are generally popular. If you find chickweed growing in your garden, keep it well watered and weed around it. I would never pick wild foods elsewhere, for the fear of contamination—fouling by animals, spraying from pesticides and even lead poisoning from weeds growing along roadsides. I also grow spinach beet (perpetual spinach) from seed; it is easy to grow and can be picked and planted through many months of the year. In the U.K., it can be planted from March to July for summer use, or in August and September for winter and spring use. It can be grown in a window box if protected from extremes of climate. Canary seed is also easy to grow. The heads can be fed green or ripe. A parrot which has never been offered greenfood may ignore it; be persistent and eventually it may be sampled—or attach it to a favourite toy. I believe that most parrots do not receive enough green leaves.

Offering fresh-cut branches from fruit trees, containing leaves and buds, may start the habit of eating green leaves. These must be washed well in case they have been contaminated by the droppings of wild birds. They could contain worm eggs; this is unlikely but possible. Few parrots can resist tender young buds. Another way of producing growing plants is to throw the leftover seed on a plot of earth and cover with soil. However, sunflowers will not ripen unless the weather is hot and dry. If it is too wet the heads will go mouldy; on no account feed in this condition.

Lito, the author's Amazon, enjoying chickweed. Almost all parrot species relish it.

Sprouting

Sprouted foods are extremely valuable, nutritionally. They contain more protein and vitamins, and less fat. For example, a sprouted lentil contains 300 percent more Vitamin C than the dry lentil. The diet of a bird that is addicted to sunflower seed can be enormously improved by offering sprouted sunflower. However, a warning must be given regarding soaked and sprouted seeds. In a warm climate, they rapidly attract the growth of bacteria and moulds. This can apparently be prevented by soaking for 20 minutes in vinegar water or citrus bioflavonoid stabiliser. Sprouted seeds must be fed in small quantities; obviously, they spoil more quickly than those which are dry (and lifeless). Mung beans and lentils, as well as sunflower seed, are suitable for sprouting. A salad sprouter can be used.

Food treats

In the U.S.A., which has an enormous industry catering for the needs of parrot owners, many wonderful food treats have been developed. One company makes special snacks to which water is added; they are then microwaved. For example, one contained bread, pumpkin, cinnamon, raisins, almonds and non-fat powdered milk. While such foods are not yet available in Europe, it is worth perusing the food section of large pet stores because the variety of foods offered for sale continues to increase. Another company has a product containing "50 thrilling natural ingredients" such as fennel seeds, pasta, ginger, four kinds of peppers, pistachios, cashews, brown rice, herbs, squash seeds and dried fruits.

Various items obtained at a health food store can be added to a parrot mixture.

In fact, anyone could make up their own on a visit to a whole foods store, adding pumpkin seeds and cooked garbanzo beans, for example. This is an excellent way to make a standard parrot mixture more interesting. However, look at the labels on the packets! Bear in mind the fat content. Here is an example of what you might buy to add to say 5 kilos (11 lb.) of parrot mixture:

500 g (1.1 lb.)	of honey-dipped banana chips
500 g (1.1 lb.)	of pumpkin seeds
500 g (1.1 lb.)	of broken mixed nuts (walnuts, hazels and cashews)
500 g (1.1 lb.)	of chick peas (to be cooked)
400 g (13.5.oz)	of Jordan's Crunchy—Tropical Fruits—toasted oat clusters (with papaya, coconut, banana and mango in small quantities)

The weight of these items was 2.4 kg (5.5 lb.) and the cost (August 1997) was £7·57 (US$12). Compare this with the same weight in best large striped sunflower, which cost about £4.50 (US$7). Before adding them to the mixture look at the analysis given.

	% protein	% carbohydrate	% fat	% fibre
Honey dipped banana chips	1.0	59.9	31.4	1.1
Pumpkin seeds	24.4	15.2	45.6	5.3
Mixed nuts	15.3	7.7	62.2	4.2
Chick peas (dry analysis)	21.4	45.2	5.4	10.7
Crunchy—Tropical Fruits	8.4	68.8	14.7	6.3

Compare these with sunflower (approximate values):

20.0	23.0	45–50

I would suggest that all these additional items would be suitable for macaws and greys, for example, but they would need to be given sparingly to species which easily become overweight, such as Amazons.

Many of the larger parrots, such as Amazons, cockatoos and eclectus, like small seeds, especially canary and white millet. As their fat content is in the region of 3 percent or 4 percent, they should be encouraged to eat them. The small seeds which are high in fat (about 45 percent to 52 percent) are niger, maw, hemp and rape. These should be avoided for pet birds, although generally hemp seed is popular.

Vitamin additives

If a vitamin and mineral additive is necessary, add it to a favourite food item, such as a grape or soft food. Do not add it to the drinking water. It is impossible to control the dose in water because one does not know how much the bird will drink; if it alters the taste or colour of the water, the parrot may not drink at all; it can obtain moisture from fruits and vegetables. Also, vitamins have a very short potency when added to water. And the parrot might bathe in the water, resulting in sticky plumage. If your bird needs extra Vitamin A, an effective method would be to pick young leaves of dandelion from your garden (no garden is without them!), wash and offer. Dandelion leaves have a very high Vitamin A content.

Remember that if 50 percent or more of your parrot's diet consists of pellets or extruded foods, supplementation with vitamins, calcium and minerals will not be necessary. These items are included. An excess of certain vitamins and of calcium can be dangerous.

Grit and cuttlefish bone

Some years ago it was accepted that parrots and parrakeets needed grit, which was usually available. Now a myth seems to have evolved that grit is dangerous and can cause compaction. The fact is that all seed-eating parrots need grit or some hard substance in order to assist the grinding of hard foods in the gizzard. However, if they exist on processed foods such as pellets, this will not be necessary. In the wild, parrots in Australia pick up grit from roadsides. It is interesting that even the nectar-feeding lorikeets are known to do so on occasions. After all, their diet includes some harder items. Many captive seed-eating parrots survive without grit because they are offered branches for chewing and swallow small pieces, or they gnaw at woodwork or even brickwork. If they do not have these opportunities I believe that a small amount of bird grit should be available. Little grit is eaten

81

Large macaws, such as the blue and yellow, need high-fat foods such as nuts.

by most species, but it should be renewed on a regular basis. I believe that the myth that grit causes compaction of the gizzard arose from the fact that sick birds with digestive problems may gorge themselves on grit. On autopsy a compacted gizzard is seen and the grit is believed to have caused the death. Healthy birds will swallow a very small amount.

Cuttlefish bone is a good source of calcium. However, unless the bird's diet contains sufficient Vitamin D3 or the bird has exposure to sunlight (enabling it to synthesise Vitamin D), it cannot absorb the calcium. Some parrot owners may believe that if their bird consumes cuttlefish bone, it cannot be calcium deficient. Of course, this is not true. Although many parrots like to destroy cuttlefish bone for the enjoyment of crunching it up, little is swallowed. It has been suggested that in these times of increasing pollution, cuttlefish bone is dangerous because it could accumulate high levels of toxins, especially heavy metals. However, except in the case of laying females, the amount of cuttlefish bone consumed by most birds is small.

Daily feeding routine
Fresh food and water must be given daily and the containers washed in hot, soapy water. It may be necessary to change the water more than once daily if the parrot dunks his food in it. Feed the basic diet as early in the morning as possible; your parrot is waiting for his breakfast! Feed additional tid-bits, fruit, nuts or an

item of human food, on two or three other occasions during the day. He will look forward to these treats and they help to create a bond between parrot and owner. In the late evening, remove uneaten items of fresh food from the cage.

Feeding young parrots

Many people do not realise that young parrots eat much more than adults until they are about nine months old. Do not ration their food: allow them to eat as much as they want. Although they may not grow much in length during this period, they do fill out over a period of many months. If their food supply is limited at this time, they may never reach the full size of their species.

Chapter 9

Toys and amusement

The importance of toys for parrots must not be underestimated. More than almost any other bird in captivity, parrots have a great need to be continually nibbling and gnawing. If they are kept on perches of hard wood there is nothing destructible in the cage except their feathers. It used to be said that feather-plucking was caused by boredom; while this was a gross oversimplification of the problem, parrots that have plenty with which to amuse themselves are less likely to pluck.

Parrots also need visual stimulation. If we were confined to one room and saw an unchanging view every day, we would be bored. We can help to alleviate their boredom by making small changes to the cage and immediate surroundings. Note the words of Phoebe Greene Linden (1997): "Once the adult parrot has a secure and comfortable hiding place, we can start fussing with the cage interior to add interest, stimulation and change...we add whole bunches of damp greens tied to the side of the cage. We add toys, and change them frequently. We create a veritable jungle of interesting items to see. It doesn't matter at all if adult parrots play with or eat these things. We are only asking the birds to be curious at this point—they don't have to participate.... If they rather haughtily skirt around an offending bunch of carrot tops or a skewer full of fresh vegetables, at least they have had to look at new things, make decisions, and think of new ways to navigate their cage. Progress is achieved."

Fortunately, today those catering for the pet trade have produced an enormous range of toys for parrots. I would especially recommend those made from wood and rope, as they are more natural than acrylic ones. However, individual birds have their preferences, for colour, form and content. Orange and pink are popular colours (a fact also noted in choice of foods). I once watched a friend who spends large sums on parrot toys, bring out a big box filled with them for her grey. What did he chose? A small plastic pill box which had cost nothing! One could make suitable toys at little cost or spend a lot on complicated ones. As with a child, there is no guarantee that a parrot will approve of your choice! Some companies in North America produce "species specific toys developed through research and aviary tests." They incorporate "colour, texture and safe materials to encourage natural inquisitiveness and foraging behaviour." These few words sum up a good toy. Safety is of great importance. If metal is used, for preference this should be steel, not zinc. And if it is made of plastic, it is not suitable for a cockatoo or macaw or any other species with a beak strong enough to break it. Obviously, there should be no open links or sharp surfaces.

Anyone who is unaware of the large range of toys available should visit a large pet store. Some toys are actually puzzles; for example, a parrot might have to undo several links to remove the nut inside it. Such toys can be recommended because they can amuse a parrot for a long period. Swings and rope ladders are excellent because they encourage activity. Young birds of almost any parrot species will soon learn to use a swing, if presented with one at the weaning stage. These can provide so much pleasure. In a large cage, a knotted skipping rope (with unvarnished handles) will provide hours of activity. If two or three toys are hung from the roof in close proximity, the inventiveness in playing with them has to be seen to be believed! I had a black-capped lory who was kept on his own for some months before a mate was found for him. He was lonely and bored and started to pluck the feathers from his thigh. Then I gave him a small wooden hammer which hung from the roof by a chain and another small piece of wood on a chain. He would spend long periods every day inventing games with them and ceased to pluck his feathers.

Toys may also help a parrot to feel secure. Donna Rosano wrote: "The placement of hanging toys can go a long way in creating security for a sensitive parrot ... I have found that hanging one or two toys in front of the favoured perches against the bars will allow the parrot to think that he is not seen. In effect, this is

Above: A huge range of parrot toys and perches is available from a good pet store.

Right: Combining toys and rope perch gives much amusement to this male red-bellied parrot.

creating a jungle like atmosphere for him where he will have multiple items to shield him from (perceived) predators." (Rosano, 1996.)

Try to match the toy to the species. As I wrote of Poicephalus, they "are active birds that enjoy all kinds of toys; these take up cage space. Swings, small cardboard boxes, small bells, cotton rope ladders and more expensive parrot toys with leather, beads and rope. However, the small species generally do not like the larger toys. Val Moat keeps her young birds amused with simple yet inexpensive ideas. Her birds do not like rawhide leather hung up in strips, yet thin strips threaded through the cage bars keep them amused for a long time. Short lengths of string (no more than six inches long) are tied to the cage bars; the strands are teased open and nibbled at. Since they are short, they are quite safe; longer lengths could be dangerous. She also hangs healthy treats from the cage roof. Toys that incorporate food are always popular!

"When I was curator at Palmitos Park, I would save the cardboard middles from toilet paper rolls for the young Red-bellied Parrots that were housed in a suspended cage outside my office

Play gyms with chains, rings and a multitude of perches can keep a parrot entertained for hours.

window. They were items for rapid destruction, except in the case of one young female. She would immediately place the roll over her head, wearing it like a huge hat that covered her eyes. She would then stagger about, totally unable to see where she was going. She would do this every time so there was no doubt that she enjoyed this strange form of amusement! It was a hilarious sight for any human observers!" (Low, 1997.)

A word of warning must be given here. Ensure that the size of the cardboard roll is larger than the bird's head, or much smaller. This will prevent an accident occurring with the roll wedged on to his head. Also ensure that ropes are not a danger. Those which are hanging with a free end should be knotted along the length to make it difficult for the rope to become twisted around the bird's neck.

The so-called play gym is popular with many parrots. Instead of spending much time in their cage, they can, especially if they have clipped wings, spend several hours a day on a stand that has been constructed with added features for exercise and entertainment. Some gyms have chains, rings and perches of irregular shape to exercise the muscles in the feet. The larger ones are on castors, so that they can easily be moved, and the smaller ones are designed as table top models. One make even has a lifetime warranty against bird damage!

The aesthetically pleasing

There is no doubt in my mind that parrots enjoy looking at objects that are aesthetically pleasing, especially if those objects belong to the natural world. Tigerlily Jones, from California, is one of those rare people who truly understands parrots. She is an artist and has an artist's eye for beauty and detail. Her article entitled "Connoisseur Conures" is one of the most moving descriptive pieces I have ever read on parrots. I will quote at length because I believe her rare insight will help others to understand that parrots appreciate the aesthetically pleasing.

"A few years back, as I was making the transition from pet-person to bird breeder, I shared my living space with three cherry headed conures. One spring day I heard a new sound that all three birds were making. Not the usual raucous calls, it was a soft purring moan. Although I would not realise it until later (when I paired up my pets) there was similarity between this sound and conure love-making. However, all three birds were in their separate cages, not even grooming each other. It was not quite a sexual noise, for it remained subdued and followed an irregular rhythm. Still, I recognised it as unmistakable sound of ecstatic pleasure, because it bore an uncanny resemblance to a sound I had heard many times while working as a sales assistant at the Highlight Gallery. Tourists...did not expect to find this type of

Use your imagination and a simple toy can be transformed into a constant delight!

Ensure that toys have no sharp edges and do not contain toxic materials. This is a safe toy —wooden items on a stainless steel chain, hung by a link that screws closed.

quality in a small rural town.... It was this sound which I now heard in my conures' voices. But what could be inspiring it?

"Curious, I went to the room where their cages hung. All three birds were facing away from me, looking out a large window which ran the length of their cages. For the moment, they were quiet; then they started up again, each with a slightly different timing and length of call, but in unison. A faint fluttering motion outside caught my eye. At first I thought it was a bevy of insects, little butterflies perhaps. I moved closer to the window, but they were gone.... Just then, a gust of wind came up and shook loose a shower of apple petals.

"Ah! Ahhh!..." led the conure to the right, closest to the tree. "Oh! Oooooo, orrr" chimed in the one in the middle as the pink and white petals fluttered in front of her. "Uhm, hmmm, mmmm...mmm" the bird on the left joined in the chorus, holding onto the note as the petals slowly descended to the lawn. Another breeze sprung up and the improvisional tune was repeated, with slight adjustments made for the strength of the wind, the amount of petals airborne, and the length of time they stayed aloft....

"They bent forward on their branches, craning their necks, anticipating the arrival of more flower petals blown their way..." (Jones, 1997.)

Fresh branches

As we cannot provide a tree, the next best thing is a branch with leaves and buds. Parrots which have not been used to these may react nervously at first. To start with, provide a leafy twig, with buds if possible, and gradually increase the size. First the buds will be sought, then the bark will be stripped. Soon it will be totally destroyed. It is worth emphasising just how much pleasure a fresh-cut piece of tree branch provides. The bark may also be providing nutrients which are lacking from the diet. Anyone who can provide fresh-cut pieces of branch on a daily basis will have a contented parrot. Gnawing is so very important, especially for cockatoos, macaws and Amazons—but all species benefit. A good branch provides occupation for hours. A parrot has a

Gus the grey parrot was offered a huge box of toys. What did he choose? A plastic pill box!

great need to gnaw. If this need is ignored it may start to pluck its own feathers or throw down its food dishes. It desperately needs occupation for the beak! This will also help to keep the beak in good condition.

Which tree branches are safe? is a very common question. First of all, they should not have been sprayed with a pesticide, which is why they should be obtained only from a known locality. They should also be washed because disease or parasites could be passed on from wild birds. In Europe the following tree species are commonly used: apple, pear, walnut, poplar, oak and elm. In the U.S.A., maple, oak and wild mustard can be added to that list. Wherever the introduced *Casuarina equisetifolia* occurs (California, for example), this is an excellent choice, especially when laden with the small seed-containing cones. Most pine trees, including spruce, are safe but those containing much sap should be avoided as they are sticky and will stain the plumage. Pine cones make the very best natural toys for parrots, who will delight in shredding them. They should be washed first. The species mentioned have fairly hard wood. If soft wood is offered, it will not last long but will be equally enjoyed. They include willow, mulberry, guava and hibiscus. Mention of the latter reminds me that flowers can also be offered, especially to the lories who will enjoy the pollen. At first they might be alarmed by the bright colours. Not all flowers are safe but hibiscus is, as are the blossom from fruit trees and catkins. It should never be forgotten that by

90

offering branches and flowers we are, in fact, providing almost the only natural items of diet which most parrots ever receive.

Most cages are not large enough to contain more than a small branch, so the following idea might be used. Cut a large branch, preferably with a horizontal side branch. Fill a flower pot of appropriate size (to take the weight) with concrete and set the branch in the wet concrete. When the concrete is dry your bird has an inexpensive alternative to his cage. When it needs renewing, it is cheap and easy to make another.

A rubbing stick

A parrot (Group A) kept alone must miss a partner to preen his plumage more than almost anything. But provided with a suitable projecting item, he will spend hours rubbing his head on it. It is a good item to cut a small branch and wedge it between the cage bars in such a way that the end projects slightly into the cage. This will make a wonderful rubbing stick.

Years ago I kept a black-headed caique (*Pionites melanocephala pallida*) as a pet. I wrote of him, that when given wood from a fruit tree: "An area of the branch is immediately stripped of bark and the body is rubbed, cat-like, against it, first on one side, then on the other. So absorbed does the bird become in these vigorous, almost frantic, rubbing movements, that I am invariably reminded of a bird anting.... If I held a twig vertically, my Pallid Caique would rub himself against it for minutes at a time, and would even sharpen the end to a point with his beak to obtain a more satisfying effect." (Low, 1972.)

The caring parrot owner will ensure that his or her parrot does not equate being returned to his cage with boredom. Remember that toys should be rotated and fresh gnawing material should be offered on a regular basis. These actions will go a long way to keeping a parrot contented.

Chapter 10

Biting—find the cause!

Biting is a common problem, and one which often leads to a family selling their bird. They cannot cope. What they have failed to realise is that when a parrot bites it is nearly always the fault of the person handling it. My female yellow-fronted Amazon has been my pet for more than 30 years at the time of writing. We therefore know each other very well. She is a well behaved bird who I handle every day. Occasionally she will bite me—not hard, but enough to make her displeasure known. When she bites me it is my fault in the cases of reasons 1) and 2) because I have broken her rules. She bites for three different reasons. 1) I have invaded her space. 2) She is jealous of my dog. 3) She is cleaning her beak on a garment of my clothing. This is a bad habit which I can easily avoid by not letting her out of her cage immediately after she has eaten an item such as a cooked vegetable which will adhere to her beak.

Although we have enjoyed such a long and happy relationship there is one action that she will not tolerate—a hand in her cage. The only exception is when I bring her out; in this case I place my hand immediately in front of her legs and she steps on. But if I want to do something to the inside of her cage I must take her out first. If I do not she will bite me. In other words, she is very possessive of her cage. If someone touches it she will lunge at them. Not all parrots behave in this way; learning the quirks of each individual is important.

The second reason she bites is out of jealousy. She does not want a rival for my attention. Occasionally my dog will jump up on to the sofa when she is on my hand. The dog comes close for a caress and the Amazon will bite me. This is a case of displaced aggression. She really wants to bite the dog; she cannot do so, therefore she bites me. However, on one occasion when my attention was not fully on my Amazon, she quickly reached down and bit the dog's ear. This was totally unacceptable behaviour, especially as the dog was asleep. I told the Amazon "No!" and immediately returned her to her cage. She is very well aware that this behaviour is wrong but on that occasion could not resist the temptation to bite the dog.

Solving the biting problem is dependent on one factor: understanding your bird. Parrots bite most often out of lack of discipline, fear, jealousy, territorial defence, neglect, as a result of being teased and, in mature birds, during what should be their breeding season. It is vitally important that biting should be stopped from the outset; if it is not, a relationship based on love and trust is totally impossible. The owner will fear the bird and the bird will be confused and lack respect for his owner. A bird who is permitted to bite his owner sees himself as dominant over that person. He believes he can do anything he wishes to do. At about six months old many hand-reared birds start to try to assert their dominance. If he is not disciplined at this age, the relationship is doomed. It will not be long before the bird is permanently confined to his cage, to spend a miserable life, lacking the close bond with another creature which he desperately needs.

Many owners of young, hand-reared parrots make the mistake of letting them nibble their fingers or pull at their fingers in play. When very young they do not normally bite hard; they are just exploring. Right from the start biting at fingers, even though it doesn't hurt, should not be permitted. It is difficult to teach a six-month-old parrot that biting fingers is wrong, when up to that time it was right!

The other point which should be known is that a parrot is aware if someone is afraid of it. I have heard of several stories of parrots who had bitten someone being permanently confined to the cage and virtually ignored. Then one day along came someone who loved and respected parrots. He or she put a hand in the cage. The bird stepped on and allowed itself to be stroked and handled without any kind of aggression. "Amazing!" said the onlookers in disbelief. No—not amazing; just a neglected bird

93

desperate for some sympathetic attention from someone who was emitting the right vibes. This would be a person who was quiet and calm, with careful movements and nothing threatening in his or her behaviour.

In this chapter I will discuss the most usual causes of biting. First, however, we need to define what is meant by a bite. I would define it as closing the mandibles with malicious intent! A young hand-reared parrot who is learning about his environment will nibble at everything within his reach. He is testing objects, for taste and texture. First he will nibble or test with his tongue, then as he grows he will bite harder. This action is, in fact, testing; it is not carried out for malicious reasons. However, he will soon discover that by biting he evokes a strong reaction from you. In other words, a way of attracting your attention! So the first rule is never to respond with a loud yelp or by shouting at him. Calmly withdraw your finger, hold up your index finger, look him in the eye and firmly say "No!" If he does it again return him to his cage immediately. If you allow him to bite you, you are reinforcing a behaviour pattern which will be very difficult to reverse at a later date. If he bites when he is on your hand, immediately assert your authority by giving the "Up!" command. If he bites when he is on your knee, it may be because you are giving your attention to someone else. If you must speak to someone at this time, do so while still looking at your bird, so that he thinks he has your full attention.

Where malicious biting is concerned, the first step is to understand the causes. In order to do so one has to realise that a parrot is a sensitive creature, with likes and dislikes and—yes—moods. He might not always feel like coming out of his cage when you want to take him out. Perhaps it is too late in the day and he wants to sleep. Disturb him at the wrong time and you may be rewarded with a nip, even though he is normally friendly. I once received this question from a parrot owner: "My parrot is hand tame but he tries to bite me if I rub his head. What should I do?" The answer was very short: Don't rub his head. If he does not want his head rubbed, why do it? However, when a relationship between bird and owner is a new one, the owner should not

94

assume the right to rub the bird's head. This right is based on trust in many cases, and if the bird does not trust you he will not allow you to rub his head.

Lesson 1. Your parrot will bite if you are performing what he sees as unreasonable behaviour. This includes any sudden movement or any other action which he perceives as threatening. So just stop and think before you fling out your arm or suddenly point at something!

Lesson 2. Your parrot may bite you if someone else is performing or has been performing unreasonable behaviour. This includes teasing by children. They MUST be made to understand that this must not happen. Unfortunately, it might happen in your absence and you are not aware of the fact. It will make your bird very nervous and therefore prone to biting when you handle him. He will view human behaviour as unpredictable and will therefore be afraid. In my view, a parrot should not be kept in a home which includes children who cannot behave responsibly toward the bird. If all other reasons for biting have been ruled out and you suspect your children, you might leave a cassette recorder recording when your children are alone in the room with the parrot. It might provide the answer.

A parrot might find its immediate environment filled with fearful items. This is especially the case with grey parrots, for some have a very nervous temperament. The cage might be too close to a television set or to a computer screen on which there are constantly moving objects, such as from a computer game. Unless the room is very large, a parrot should not be kept in the same room as a TV or computer. The flashing lights from both create a confusing and disturbing environment. This is especially the case where the television is never turned off until the family goes to bed.

Lesson 3. Don't keep a sensitive species like a grey in an entertainment centre. Few parrots could adapt to this.

Lesson 4. Don't give out signals of fear. If a parrot is trained to step on to the hand, he will do so immediately if approached in a positive manner. In other words, direct the hand toward the bird's lower breast, at medium speed; don't hesitate! If the hand wavers in the cage, the parrot will reach up or down and bite the hand. I have seen this happen on countless occasions. The bird is not a biter in the malicious sense. He is merely warding off an intrusive object. He will not do this if your intention to take him out is clear.

Lesson 5. Some birds are naturally aggressive, even if they have been hand-reared. The first which comes to mind in this category is the female eclectus. I have hand-reared many. Some have a pleasant temperament. Others lunge and bite. Those which I have reared which have behaved in this way were destined as breeding birds; they were not handled after they were independent so no attempt was made to correct this behaviour. Thenceforth it did not occur because they were in an aviary. The problem starts even before they are weaned, that is, when one puts one's hand inside the cage to remove them to be fed. I could not recommend such individuals of the species as pets. There are plenty more who do not behave in this way.

Lesson 6. Placing a parrot's cage high up so that the members of the household have to look up at him, leads the parrot to believe that he is the dominant member of the household. He will not tolerate hands appearing from below and bites them. Place the cage or stand on a table or lower the level so that your eye level is higher than the bird's.

The cage is best placed in a corner or against a wall.

Lesson 7. If the parrot's cage is in the wrong place he may be constantly under stress. This applies especially to a bird which is not tame, such as a wild-caught parrot. Even a hand-reared one will suffer if people are constantly coming at it from all sides. The cage is

ʾaped Amazon (14 in.). Superb mimic; loud.

yellow-headed Amazon (14 in.). Excellent talker; noisy.

Above: Orange-winged Amazon
Harsh voice.

Left: Spectacled or white-fronted Am
in.). Less talented mimic.

Opposite page: Blue-headed pionus
Usually quiet and gentle.

Young white-bellied caique (9 in.). Uncommon but playful and fearless.

Festive Amazon (13 in.). Rarely available but excellent mimic.

Hawk-headed parrot (12 in.). Beautiful but feisty.

Orange-flanked or grey-cheeked parrakeet (8 in.). Amusing and beautiful.

te top: Wagler's conure (15 in.).
nate and playful—but loud.

te bottom: Young golden-crowned or
ronted conure (10 in.). Very attractive.

Lesser Patagonian conures (18 in.).
ul, affectionate and intelligent—but noisy.

Green-cheeked conures (10 in.). Very pop-
s when hand-reared.

te top: Green-winged macaw
). Intelligent and affection-
ut loud and demanding.

te bottom left: Yellow-naped
(16 in.). Playful, intelligent
table size.

te bottom right: Green-naped
(11 in.). Playful and affec-
if hand-reared.

Umbrella cockatoos (18 in.).
onally demanding and sensi-
ds.

Young military macaw (30
ss popular as pets, yet inter-
and affectionate.

Red lory (11 in.). Beautiful; can talk but fairly loud.

Black-capped lory (12 in.). Amusing and good mimic but piercing voice.

Above: Eclectus male (14 in.). Beautiful; good mimic but can be noisy.

Left: Red-sided eclectus female (14 in.). Exquisite plumage; some of uncertain temperament.

Masked lovebirds (6 in.). Best kept in true pairs.

Grey parrot (13 in.). Renowned mimic; needs a very caring owner.

rrot. Young birds are recognized by dark eyes.

lied female (9 in.). Strong-willed and tend to be one-person pets.

Left: Cockatiel (12 in.). Ma
tions available; males are
talkers.

Below: A young brown-
parrot (9 in.). Sweet tempe

Opposite top: Jardine's pa
in.). Beautiful and, I
Poicephalus, can be good r

Opposite below: Young J
parrot. Duller in colour and
beak than adult.

Above: Alexandrine parrak
in.). Intelligent and beaut
destructive and not affectior

Left: Young galah (roseate
breasted) cockatoo (14 in.).

Below: Adult galah. B
plumage.

best placed in a corner or against the wall between two pieces of furniture. This provides a sense of security because the cage can be approached only from one or two sides. The worst position would be a cage which could be approached on four sides. The bird could be under constant stress, thus would bite out of fear.

Lesson 8. A hard one to take: your parrot might not like you. You might be blameless; perhaps you remind him of someone who ill-treated him in the past. Or the problem may be simply that you are your partner's partner and your bird has bonded to your partner. He is jealous of the attention you give to and receive from his favourite person. While he may learn to tolerate you, it is rather unlikely that you will ever become his favourite person! This is very hard to take if the parrot was originally intended to be yours. The best way to behave is simply to avoid confrontations. When your partner has the bird out of the cage, do not be present in the same room. When your partner is not in the house, talk to the parrot and try to establish some kind of bond, without trying to handle him.

Lesson 9. Your parrot's behaviour may change during the breeding season when his hormone levels rise. Males are the most difficult to deal with at this time; in fact, they may become dangerous. A male cockatoo, macaw or Amazon may run around the floor trying to nip toes or ankles. Or he may dive-bomb you. There is no other way to deal with this than to confine him to his cage. You might even consider building an indoor or outdoor aviary so that he can be placed inside for the period when he becomes too difficult to handle. The larger parrots are capable of inflicting a severe injury. If this happens, the owner may be too afraid to handle the bird again. This behaviour is not the bird's fault. If he must be confined to his cage he should receive plenty of attention and tidbits so that the bond between bird and owner is maintained.

On the subject of food, one hopes that such a situation would never occur, but a bird which was consistently underfed might start to bite as soon as he was let out of his cage. Many people do not realise how much food a young parrot needs. This is especially true of macaws. Such birds might unintentionally be underfed.

Lesson 10. Many wild-caught parrots have suffered terribly during capture and transport. As a result, they are terrified of hands. They will never accept human hands near them. To approach such a bird, put your hands behind your back. If it is responsive and fairly friendly, talk to it close to the cage. Do this often, never showing your hands, and the day may come when it allows you to rub its head using your nose. This is because parrots seem to equate the human nose with their beak. A warning must be issued here! If you misjudge the bird's reaction it could disfigure you for life, by biting your nose. Only an experienced and sensitive person should use this technique. I used it successfully with a wild-caught male citron-crested cockatoo. Another, safer method, after you have won the trust of such a bird, is to use a short length of twig to rub its head. Eventually you may be able to dispose of the twig.

Lesson 11. Some parrots have long memories. If you abuse them in any way, do not expect them to forget. Tom Spence recounted the story of his pair of purple-naped lories (*Lorius domicellus*). They had the freedom of his office. One day he was called away suddenly. When he returned it was to find that they were "making confetti of a small fortune in National Insurance stamps. When I seized the male somewhat roughly to return him to his cage, he bit me savagely and has sought to do so ever since...." (Spence, 1955). How had he behaved previously? He was "very, very tame and when he moulted into adult plumage and the pair were brought together the two would sit, one on each shoulder, fondling my ears and murmuring love-words to me...."

Displaced aggression was mentioned at the beginning of this chapter. A common scenario is as follows: the parrot is sitting on the man's shoulder. His child suddenly runs up and frightens the bird. As the parrot cannot bite the child, he bites the nearest object to his beak, which is the man. As this is a reflex action there is no point in trying to discipline the bird. Its reaction will always be the same, given these circumstances. It is not the bird whose behaviour needs correcting, but the child's.

Where the bird is at fault the reaction should always be a stern "No!" with eye contact, with immediate return to the cage. If your parrot bites while he is inside his cage, the fault lies with you.

What should you do if a previously well-behaved parrot suddenly starts to bite you? I have no experience of such a case, but parrot behaviourists suggest the following. Take the parrot to a room away from his cage, every day for ten to 15 minutes. Your aim will be to retrain him in reacting to verbal commands. If he is already obedient to the "Up!" and "Down!" commands, teach him something new. In so doing you are re-establishing your position as the one who is in control.

The most difficult parrots to cure of biting are adult birds which have been mistreated in their previous home. It may take a long time to obtain their trust. Patience and gentleness are the keywords. When such a bird realises that you are consistently kind you will have a friend for life.

Chapter 11

To clip or not to clip?

The most controversial issue surrounding the ownership of pet parrots is whether or not their wings should be clipped—unless, of course, you live in the U.S.A. There it is standard practice. Although there are certain circumstances in which it might be advisable to clip a pet parrot's wings on a permanent basis, in most instances this concept is totally unacceptable to me.

Most keepers of parrots who have the wings of their birds clipped do so because they fear it might escape. Sadly, over the years, I have known about countless cases where pet parrots have escaped. Ironically, most of them relate to birds which had been clipped. This act tends to give the owners a false sense of security; they either forget to check the condition of the primaries or they do not realise that a parrot can fly if it has as few as two or three primaries in each wing. Incredibly, I have even heard of new owners who believed that once the wing feathers were clipped, the bird would never fly again.

Many times I have heard the lament: "I didn't know he could fly!" after a cherished pet has escaped. This is because a bird which has had its flights cut over a long period ceases to try to fly. But should it be frightened suddenly, it instinctively takes off. Many parrots can fly with unimpaired speed and accuracy with only half their complement of wing feathers. If you have one which is clipped, you MUST check its flight feathers at two-month intervals or as soon as you see a moulted cut feather on the floor.

Wing-clipping does not necessarily prevent escape—so why do it? I cannot think of any good reason. In my opinion, pet parrots should be allowed out of their cage only under supervision; there are too many hazards and escape is only one of them. The owners of full-winged birds pay constant attention to what their bird is doing during its period of relative freedom—which is as it should be. Most parrots enjoy the power of flight so much (limited though it is, of necessity), that it seems heartless to deprive them.

I can think of several important reasons why parrots should not have their wings clipped.

1. It damages them physically and psychologically.
2. It can lead to injury as a result of falling.
3. It can result in infection or tumours.
4. The stress of wing-clipping often triggers feather-plucking, especially in grey parrots (*Psittacus erithacus*).

Some owners allow their wing-clipped birds to sit on the top of the cage. The bird may be under stress because of the constant fear of falling; this is especially the case with birds which are not tame, such as wild-caught grey parrots. Vets report seeing parrots with split tissue on the breast or abdomen or below the cloaca, as a result of constant falling on to a hard surface. It is difficult to believe that there are owners who show so little concern—but sadly, such people do exist. Because the owner has not noticed—possibly when a parrot falls repeatedly from its perch on to the cage floor—a bacterial infection develops.

Julie Hamilton, who runs a parrot rescue centre in the U.K., reported: "We are receiving young birds that are debilitated through severe wing-clipping. One two-year-old African Grey arrived at the Rescue with a severe, protruding scab on the surface of his breast bone—caused by crash landing into a hard object. The accident happened a year ago, and if it had been a slight injury it would have healed by now. He was seen by a vet who informed the owner it was nothing to worry about and quite normal!" Julie Hamilton consulted an avian vet who treated the grey with an antibiotic to clear the deep-rooted infection. (Hamilton, 1997.)

Falling can also result in broken tail feathers which often lead to the unfortunate bird plucking the new feathers as they grow, due to the irritation an infection causes. An infection may occur when the broken feather shaft is forced into the skin as the result of another fall.

In one collection where a number of macaws are exhibited to the public with clipped wings, several had tumours on the wings. This was apparently the result of many years of repeated wing-clipping. One breeder, Elaine Froggatt, who rears greys, was in the habit of clipping the wings of her young birds. Then she had a problem. The feathers of one grey which had been clipped, were not moulted. There was irritation in the area and the grey chewed the feathers and the skin. An infection set in and hard nodules formed around the base of the old feathers. The dead feathers were carefully removed with small pliers. When new feathers grew, they dropped out when only half formed, with blood quills.

At this point veterinary advice was sought and the opinion was that there was no blood supply to the skin inside the feather cavity supporting the feather shaft. Therefore the feather was falling out before it was fully developed. The vet prescribed a course of hormones, Ovarid (5 mg) to nourish the follicles and restore the blood supply to growing feathers. Initially half a tablet was crushed in a teaspoon and taken with liquid twice a week. This treatment was successful and the grey's plumage was eventually perfect—but not until after it had suffered a long period of stress. (Hormone treatment helps African Grey by "special correspondent", *Bird Keeper*, December 1996, page 56.)

One lady wrote to me about her 14-month-old Senegal parrot. She obtained him from a friend who tired of him when he started to pluck himself. She sent me a photograph of the Senegal from which I was appalled to see the manner in which his wings had been clipped—or should I say butchered? The lady who rescued him wrote: "He has calmed down physically from the nervous, twitchy little bird who would not stop picking at his feathers, even to eat." In her caring ownership, he should be full-winged again and hopefully unrecognisable in the beauty of his plumage.

Today, the practice of clipping the wings of young, hand-reared parrots, is becoming more common. Almost as soon as they are weaned, they are deprived of the power of flight. In addition to not allowing them to exercise in the most natural way, it

This Senegal was wing-clipped in a cruel and inappropriate manner. It resulted in him feeling insecure and led to feather plucking.

probably results in the pectoral muscles failing to develop properly. If the bird's flight feathers are allowed to grow, it will be a long time before it can fly well, as its pectoral muscles will take months to strengthen.

A British breeder, Greg Glendell, wrote to me: "I think the importance of letting pet birds fly is very under-estimated and poorly understood. Occasionally they like to let off steam by having a mad flying session. I'd do the same if I could! Fitness is vital to birds and I believe it makes them much more resistant to infections and minor ailments if they are fit. They cannot get fit (in terms of having a healthy heart and respiratory system) unless they can get exercise by flying."

This opinion is a valid one. I have never clipped the wings of a young parrot. I know instinctively that it is wrong. Therefore I cannot speak from personal experience regarding the psychological effect of this act.

However, on the subject of parrots at the weaning stage, Kelly Tucker wrote: "Parrots who cannot fly at this stage of their development become anxious and fearful. They may become fixated on a particular food, bowl or bowl placement. They may become extremely phobic, nervous or self-mutilating." (Tucker, 1996.)

Unfortunately, many people do not know the correct way to trim a parrot's wing feathers in order to prevent flight. If this is not carried out correctly, it is a pointless exercise—or even a cruel one. A sad case of ignorance in this respect was related by Dr

Gregory Rich at the IAS Convention in Orlando, Florida, in 1996. He showed a slide of a cockatiel which had had its wings trimmed to the bone....

These are the practical reasons why wing-clipping is wrong. We can see and measure the damage done. This is impossible in respect of the psychological damage. But it undoubtedly exists, especially in the case of wild-caught birds which had always known the power of flight. I can think of no good reason for depriving a pet bird of this natural and vital dimension. It is different in the case of an aggressive male of a breeding pair when the male must be made slightly less mobile for a limited period, for the safety of the female. I have done this myself—and have never known any unfortunate consequences. But as no pet bird should be left out of its cage unsupervised, there can be no justification for wing-clipping.

To cut its flight feathers in order to tame it, as is sometimes advocated, is deplorable, in my view. Someone showed me some discussion they had surfed on the internet (*Pet's Forum* in the U.S.A.) which appalled me. A query as to whether the owner of a grey should clip its wings was answered with the opinion: "I would not allow your Grey free flight. You lose control over him, and part of his bond to humans is due to being unable to fly. It is amazing how humble they become once grounded." Does this sound like a bird lover? Or someone who knows no other way to master a defenceless creature?

In one bird magazine, a reader asked what she could do to stop her grey from biting other people. He was well-behaved with the owner. The answer given was to clip his wings and put him on a stand. I view this as extreme punishment for something which was not the bird's fault. I would suggest the owner is more likely to have been at fault for allowing other people to handle the grey. I wouldn't think of allowing other people to handle my Amazon—because I know she would bite them. But I do not consider this to be a fault in her personality. I simply accept it. While we expect a young hand-reared parrot to go to anyone, we should not expect the same of an adult bird. In fact it is irresponsible to allow strangers to handle adult parrots, no matter how tame they are with some people, because if they do not like a person they can inflict a serious wound.

Are we so out of touch with nature that we cannot understand the psychological effect of wing-clipping? In the many islands of Indonesia, where cockatoos, lories and other parrots are caught in huge numbers to fuel the pet trade, do the natives cut the bird's wing feathers to render them flightless? No, they do not. They attach a ring, usually made of coconut shell, to the leg, and tether the bird to perches. Many of these people wear nothing more than a loin-cloth and know little about the modern world. They might be termed "savages" by some. But to my mind the term would be better applied to those who butcher the wings of parrots. Many of them hardly give a thought to whether this act is really necessary. It is not. If the owner cannot look after a parrot unless he resorts to rendering it flightless, he should not be a parrot owner.

When I voiced this opinion in the British magazine *Bird Keeper* (March 1997) most of the response came from people who agreed with me. Of course, some did not. Linda Thompson wrote to say: "My (wing-clipped) Blue-headed Pionus has a whale of a time in our house and as you can see from the photograph she is certainly not sad or depressed."

Elizabeth Lovell put forward another viewpoint. She wrote: "My family always let our hand-reared parrots learn to fly first, then we lightly clip both wings. This allows them to fly, but lower and slower." However, if a bird can fly at all, it can still escape—and if it cannot fly fast it cannot escape cats or other predators, thus the logic behind this practice is difficult to follow.

In support of my views, Pam Fryer wrote: "What is needed is more responsible owners—not wing-clipped birds. Birds have been known to start plucking their feathers due to wing-clipping, and I believe it causes many psychological problems, such as depression.... If a survey was carried out, I am sure it would be found that as many birds have died from the effects of wing-clipping as those which have flown away."

In my opinion, common sense protects most pet parrots better than wing-clipping, A bird is a wonderful flying machine and revels in that ability. If you don't want a pet that flies, buy a dog....

Chapter 12

Basic training for owner and parrot

There is one fact that the new parrot owner should understand from the outset. The larger parrots, especially cockatoos, are highly intelligent. They can be manipulative: they can manipulate you without you realising it. This is one reason why so many people encounter problems with cockatoos and why the white cockatoos (*Cacatua* species) are not suitable for those who never had a parrot before. In short, they are too clever. They soon learn how to get attention which, initially, may be by screaming. While other parrots may also soon learn this trick, they seldom do it as persistently and as loudly as do cockatoos. Those white beauties not only scream, but will reinforce their need for attention by flinging their food cups around the cage and scattering the food outside it. Unfortunately, not too many food containers are cockatoo-proof. The new owner who was tempted into the purchase of an adorable, cuddly recently weaned—or worse-still, not yet weaned—baby cockatoo may, only a few weeks later, be confronted with a screaming bird which can be pacified only by letting it out of the cage. The new parrot owner does not know how to deal with such a situation and will probably sell the cockatoo in desperation. Therefore, the very first rule that the owner must learn, FROM DAY ONE, is how to respond to his or her bird.

Unfortunately, because so many cockatoos are force-weaned at an early age, they will be very insecure and soon become demanding. Training will, through no fault of the owner, be extremely difficult in many cases. I repeat, cockatoos are not for novices with parrots. But, if they have bought one, if it is given the correct guidance and discipline from the start, it can become everything that they dreamed of.

So, the first rule is this: if your parrot is screaming for attention, don't ignore him but don't go rushing to the cage. Look up or turn round from what you are doing. Call out to him reassuringly and carry on with what you were doing. However, with that glance make sure that all is well. That he has the basic needs in his cage: food, water and a toy. If you rush to him every time he calls out, even if you are going over to the cage to tell him to be quiet, the equation in his mind is simple: Scream out = human comes running. He has manipulated you!

Parrots must be trained only with love and kindness. But they need to know, right from day one, who is in charge. You are in charge and you will take him out of the cage when it is convenient for you. I would suggest set daily periods so that your parrot knows what to expect. If you quickly establish a routine he will feel more secure, knowing that in the evening (or whatever time is best for you) he will spend perhaps 30 minutes or 60 minutes with you, when you can devote your full attention to him. At other times maintain vocal contact by speaking to him, even if only briefly, whenever you pass his cage. If there are no set daily periods, insecurity will set in. He wants your attention but has no idea when he will get it, so he screams.

Many new owners are so delighted that they initially spend long periods with their parrot, even though they know that this will not be possible on a permanent basis. This is a huge mistake. They should start as they mean to go on.

Perching on shoulders

A common mistake is to allow a parrot to perch on your head or shoulder. Most birds like to perch at the highest convenient point—convenient for them, that is! Why is this not a good idea for the owner?

1. It is difficult to remove the bird yourself—and someone else who tries to, risks being bitten because the parrot is possessive about you.

2. You need to maintain eye contact with your parrot; this is impossible.

3. The habit may start when your parrot is young and cuddly; when he is older he might find out what a wonderful reaction he gets if he bites your ear! Also, if he is possessive about you, he may bite your face if someone approaches too closely. This is a form of displaced aggression; he cannot bite the other person, so he bites you. He could also bite at or near your eye, causing a serious injury.

4. A parrot on your head or shoulder considers himself dominant over you if his eye level is above yours.

5. If you wear glasses, earrings or other jewelry, you can expect them to be damaged. They are just another parrot toy, in his view.

When you are watching television or sitting quietly with your parrot, place him on your knee or on the arm of the chair.

Stepping on the hand (the "Up!" command)

It is essential that a parrot can be moved in and out of his cage, or away from an unsuitable place, when necessary. If a parrot has to be chased around, this is a clear sign that the bird is in control. It is no basis for a relationship. Neither bird nor owner benefits. If a parrot is trained to do only one thing, it must be to step on and off the hand. It is very easy for a young bird to learn this, if he is correctly taught. It is so simple with a hand-reared parrot. Take him out of his cage—in fact, as far in the room from the cage as possible. (He considers the cage to be his territory.) Place him on his stand or on the back of a chair. Look at him kindly and move your hand at medium speed, and not jerkily, toward his abdomen. Push your index and middle finger (or index finger only in a small bird) firmly above his legs. Say "Up!" If he steps on to your hand, praise him. If he does not, gently place his feet on your fingers. You can then transfer him to your other hand, repeating "Up!" Do this three or four times. Then replace him on the stand or chair, saying "Down!" Praise him again. Repeat the process a few minutes later. Do this whenever you take him out of his cage. He will soon learn. When he does it automatically as you place your fingers above his feet, continue to say "Up!" It will not be long before he starts to step on to your hand as soon as you say "Up!" This is the first step toward a well-behaved parrot over which you have control.

When the "Up!" command is perfected, teach your parrot to step on to a perch or short length of stick. There are two advantages. If you are away and someone who is nervous of or unknown to your parrot needs to handle him, that person and your parrot will have more confidence if a small perch is used. The second point is that if you have to move your bird when he has been frightened or upset, it is safer to do so using a perch. This should prevent you from being bitten.

There may be times when it is important for you to place him in the cage quickly, to keep him out of harm. But, most importantly, he must learn that you are above him in the order of dominance. For this reason, do not leave the cage door open for him to come out when he wishes. Wait for a suitable time, then invite him to step on to your hand, using the word "Up!". If he is feeding, playing or sleeping, wait a few minutes. It is your decision when he comes out.

If he does not know, from one day to the next, who is dominant, he will become confused. Like a child, he needs guidance. If it is always given with kindness and gentleness, the relationship between bird and owner will grow into something wonderful. The trust will always be there. Your behaviour should be predictable. If you are not in a good mood and do not have the patience for a training session, defer it. If you lose your temper, you could lose your parrot's trust for ever.

Early training

In the U.K., Greg Glendell is an exceptional breeder of a small number of Timneh grey parrots and Amazons. He chooses very carefully the homes to which his young ones will go. Before they go, he trains them to obey three basic commands. These are: "On here," to step on to the hand; "Go down" to step off the hand; and a command to prevent a parrot from landing on you (as you are leaving the room for example). This is the "No" command, with one hand raised. The young birds are never allowed to land on anyone's head. If one does, he shakes his head and says "No" until it departs. It should not be removed by hand.

He tells the new owners that it is vital that the parrot obeys these commands. If it does not, the owner should contact him for advice on retraining. It is important that everyone in the house uses the commands correctly.

Most of his young birds are hand-reared. Some are parent-reared and the training applies equally to them. He told me: "Obedience training is very easy with hand-reared birds. Even before they are fledged I start to use the "On here" and "Down" commands. When they can fly, apart from the first two commands, I let them do their own thing for a couple of weeks, until they are reasonably skillful at manoeuvring in flight. At this point I introduce the "No" command and raise my hand if I don't want them to land on me for a while. Obedience in these commands is about 70–80 percent. Parent-reared birds are removed from their parents at about one to two weeks after fledging. They are not as relaxed about training but are not at all difficult. The bird should see you as a trusted friend, perhaps like an older brother or sister, but you should be above the bird in dominance."

The difficult stage

Unfortunately, many parrot owners do not teach the basic "No" command, believing it to be unnecessary. They are unaware that as the bird matures he may become more difficult to handle because he is used to getting his own way. They can expect trouble in a large parrot at the age of about two years. Tracy and Ian Lorriman have two greys, both

If your parrot is in the habit of landing in high places, train it to step on a little wooden ladder.

126

males. Tracy described their behaviour at this stage: "Gilbert was extremely temperamental for months. Ian could not put him back in his cage and we both thought he would never improve. But with a lot of patience he did improve. Now he is wonderful—with both of us—and getting better. Gus, on the other hand, only had a brief 'temper tantrum' lasting one or two weeks. I thought it was quite surprising, and indicative of the diversity in personalities, that the length of time for these difficult periods was so different."

If your bird's behaviour suddenly deteriorates, whether it is biting, screaming, plucking or not wishing to be handled, review every aspect of his care. This includes diet, showering, regular provision of fresh branches, items to play with, regular daily periods outside the cage, training reinforcement of the "Up!" command and the possibility of teasing or annoyance from family or visitors. Do this with care. Over the months or years you have had him, you may gradually have become careless in some area. If your standard of care has not deteriorated, and the change in behaviour cannot be attributed to hormonal influences in the breeding season, you might consider taking your parrot to an avian vet who has a good reputation, to perform routine tests, including a complete blood count (CBC).

Ill health does not always manifest itself in obvious outward signs, and it may be that your parrot is not in perfect health. On the other hand, perhaps he is going through a difficult period at adolescence. This does not affect all birds.

It's never too late

Is it ever too late to teach the "Up!" command? No! Shari Carpenter related how she overcame the problem with a Moluccan cockatoo, a much-loved pet who had not been disciplined. By the time he was two years old he was "out of control," screaming and aggressive. His bouts of screaming drove his owner to "the brink of insanity." But she knew that she was to blame and was determined to overcome the problem. Then she started to read articles by Sally Blanchard, who described how this could be done. The first step was to teach him the "Up!" command. He liked walking about on the floor; when he did so, she could force him to step on to her arm. Every time he stepped up he heard the word "Up!" She would then hold him close and give him the love he had always enjoyed. She did that repeatedly, until he associated the word with positive things. He associated it with approval. Once he had learned "Up!" she taught him "No!" when he had done something wrong. She wrote: "After he started accepting verbal commands his spoiled behaviour began to fade. Although he was mature, he learned UP, DOWN and NO so quickly. Our confidence in each other began to blossom."

Shari Carpenter then taught him "Up! Cage." On hearing that he would run back to his cage and climb in. It was easy to teach him this after she discovered he loved hand-clapping. He liked clapping and being the centre of attention so much that he accepted it as a reward for good behaviour. The clapping game enabled his owner to invent several games for him to play.

If only more owners would accept that they are to blame. Shari Carpenter did so without hesitation: "I'm very proud of Fagan. He has come a long way and I credit his inherent intelligence, kindness and a willingness to forgive my mistakes. Fagan has always been, and continues to be, one of the great loves of my life." (Carpenter, 1997.)

Which is the one "tool" which restores tameness to a parrot which has started to become difficult? Sally Blanchard wisely states that it is ten to 15 minutes of "focused attention a day." By focused attention she means time which is shared only between you and your parrot: you can cuddle him, scratch his head, talk to him or teach him new words or songs. That makes sense. Give him extra attention and he will respond. Perhaps you were at fault, anyway, because you had gradually, without realising it, ceased to give him the time or the quality of attention which he had been used to.

His fault or your fault?

If your parrot bites, gnaws the furniture or does something that displeases you, first ask yourself: "Whose fault was that?" Perhaps he bit you because something frightened him, or someone came too close to you. Did he gnaw the furniture because he was never properly disciplined? If you let him bite at one chair because it is old, you cannot expect him to understand that another chair is taboo. Right from the first moment he is seen to gnaw at furniture, he must be made to understand that it is not permitted. Give a firm "No!" and point with your index finger while he is doing it—not when he has stopped. If he does it again, return him to his cage. This is when the "Up!" command is useful. You cannot begin to discipline him if you cannot catch him! If you had to chase him about at this point, he would think it was some kind of game that merited a repeat performance!

Put him in his cage and walk out of the room. That is punishment. He wanted your presence and your attention and now he has lost it. ANY other form of punishment is not permissible. In their actions, the larger parrots show that they experience fear, pleasure, jealousy and many other emotions which are common to humans. (Almost certainly the smaller ones do also, but their emotions are more difficult to interpret.) When admonishing a bird, the owner should try to put himself or herself in his parrot's place. He or she is usually the centre of the parrot's world. The parrot craves affection and attention. The owner or the family is the only source of this affection, which is just as necessary to its well-being as is food and water. If a child behaved badly and the parent consulted a doctor, to be told: "Smack him and ignore him for the next two months," the parent would react with incredulity, and probably with anger, that the doctor showed so little understanding of human nature. To act in this way would severely damage the relationship, probably irreparably damage it. Yet in a book published in 1994 which is considered to be an indispensable manual for the avian vet, the advice given is as follows: "A good way to overcome negative behaviour is to avoid it. A biting bird should receive no affection (e.g., petting, holding) for one to two months." Sadly, this illustrates how little understanding even some people who work with birds on a daily basis have of parrot behaviour. Ignoring a parrot for two months will not cure biting. It would result in a lonely and frustrated bird which would probably bite even harder the next time it was handled. Any punishment, such as putting the bird in its cage then walking out of the room, should be short in its duration. Then he can be let out again. If he misbehaves again, he must be put back at once. Then the bird will associate the two actions in his mind. The first once or twice he may not do that.

Parrot behaviourists

In the U.S.A., there are a number of parrot behaviourists who give advice or train a parrot for a fee. It may be only a matter of time before such people exist in Europe. As in any profession, there are good and bad practising. However, anyone can set themselves up as a behaviourist; they do not need any letters after their name. Some of these people are excellent; others apparently have little understanding of parrot behaviour. Bad advice could result in permanent damage to the bird's personality or the relationship between parrot and owner. In just one issue of *The Pet Bird Report* two such incidents were described in different articles recounting how problems had been overcome.

One owner of two greys was determined that they would live together in the same cage. Naturally the one who had been in residence for a long time resented the newcomer. To suggest keeping them in the same cage was a recipe for disaster which only an inexperienced person would suggest unless it was absolutely obvious that the two birds wanted to be together. Where a parrot is very close to its owner, this is unlikely to happen. Yet a "behaviourist" insisted that it was possible and took the two greys and cage into his or her own home for several periods over a matter of months. When the birds were returned to the owner, the original bird would attack the newcomer, knocking her off the perch and biting at her. "Sometimes she was so terrified she would scream while huddled in a corner of the cage" but the behaviourist instructed "do nothing and let the birds work it out" (Wright, 1997). I am appalled that someone paid money for this kind of inhumane and totally incorrect advice. Apparently common sense was deferred in the belief that the behaviourist must be right. If you are not happy with advice you are given, don't follow it. It's your bird whose welfare is at stake and you know the bird better than anyone else. In this case, the grey who was constantly attacked was returned to her previous owner. Formerly sweet-natured, she came back as an aggressive, "street-smart" bully. She attacked other birds which came within 3 ft. (1 m) of her. Considering the terrifying ordeal she had been through, this was predictable.

The other story related to Fagan, the Moluccan cockatoo. When his owner was at a loss as to how to correct the problems experienced with him, she happened to meet a bird trainer who had developed a bird show. One of the problems was that the cockatoo would not stay on his stand. The man told her that when Fagan got off his stand she or her husband should pick him up at the base of his tail and place him back on his stand. Her husband, who was the cockatoo's favourite person, decided to do this. From that moment on Fagan would have nothing more to do with her husband. He would "turn his back and refuse to look at him." For 18 months the cockatoo acted as though her husband did not exist. I do not find this at all surprising. Cockatoos are very sensitive birds; I believe that their emotions are very close to our own. How could the bird possibly understand what it had done wrong? For two years it had acted in the same way without being corrected. Why should it connect its behaviour with its owner suddenly grabbing it by the base of the tail? That would be a frightening and humiliating experience for the cockatoo, who had previously known only love and gentle handling. Whatever advice he or she is given, a parrot owner MUST try to put themselves in the bird's place and question whether the advice a) is sensible; b) will cause the parrot emotional distress; c) will damage its relationship with its owner.

Someone with a problem might write to a bird magazine which has an advisory service. Having read many letters from such people I know that it is very difficult to give advice. The letter is usually short and much relevant information is missing. Often the key to the problem is not mentioned. The best way to give advice would be to watch a video which showed the bird, surroundings, owner and family—but, of course, this is not available. A person with a problem might seek advice from many different sources and receive as many different answers. They simply have not provided enough details or the right information to enable a useful reply to be given.

It is often very difficult for a new parrot owner to know what he or she is doing wrong. There is so much to learn and the owner simply does not have enough experience to deal with a sensitive and intelligent creature like a parrot. Many parrot owners have not kept any kind of bird before and know little about bird behaviour. As a result the parrot suffers due to his owner's ignorance. Then the bird is blamed unjustly. The purchase of a parrot, a grey, for example, by someone who has never previously kept birds can be compared with someone who is learning to ride buying an Arab stallion for the purpose. Problems are inevitable. I am often saddened by the questions I am asked because they show a total lack of understanding of the nature of a parrot.

Praise good behaviour

Chris Davis, a well-known parrot behaviourist in the U.S.A., emphasises the importance of praising a bird when it behaves well: "Merely praising the bird while it is behaving in an acceptable manner will teach it to repeat the same behaviour in the future. Try it! If you are consistent, you may find that your little feathered friend will gradually become better behaved.... Often, the majority of our interactions with our birds are to scold them for doing something that we do not like. The birds will treat this kind of interaction as a reward, and will continue their negative behaviours because we've trained them to do so!

"Unfortunately, we tend to send mixed messages, and most birds have had their negative behaviours rewarded so frequently that they cannot clearly understand what their people expect from them. Any time that you look at the birds, talk to them or interact with them in any way, you are rewarding them. Take care to do so only if the bird is doing something you like." (Davis, 1997.)

Simple tricks

If your bird has responded well to learning basic commands, both of you might enjoy progressing a stage further. On the other hand, you might find the idea of teaching your parrot tricks distasteful.

When your parrot is amusing himself and not being demanding, praise him. Too often all a parrot receives are negative responses from human companions.

Unquestionably, many parrots do enjoy learning and performing tricks. After all, it is a way of receiving attention and admiration. It is also a way of reinforcing the bond between you and your bird. However, if your bird does not enjoy this, do not pursue the idea. Do not do anything that will spoil the existing relationship.

Whatever you wish to teach your bird, words or tricks, this is best accomplished in a quiet room with no distractions. This means no other person should be present.

The period when parrots are easiest to train, i.e., from about one month after weaning, varies in length. It lasts perhaps up to two years in cockatoos and macaws, but for a shorter period in smaller parrots. Of course, if they have been trained on a continuing basis, they are more easily taught new tricks or words or commands. This does not mean that an older bird is untrainable, but that it will be more difficult. If the bird is not tame, it will be very difficult, perhaps impossible.

Patience is essential

Whether you wish to teach your parrot a trick or to correct some aspect of his behaviour, remember that patience and kindness are essential. Extreme patience may be needed with behavioural problems. According to Sally Blanchard, the main reason why behaviour modification fails is because the owner does not persevere long enough.

133

Chapter 13

Mimicry

I cannot claim to write this chapter from experience as I have never been interested in teaching parrots to talk. If those in my care have done so, it was because they were natural mimics, not because they received any lessons! I firmly believe that MIMICRY SHOULD NEVER BE THE MOTIVE FOR BUYING A PARROT. If someone cannot appreciate a parrot for the wonderful creature that it is, but perceives it as desirable because human words flow from its beak, he or she is not a suitable parrot owner, in my opinion.

There are a few facts which the owner of a parrot that is to be taught to talk should know.

- A parrot that is unhappy in its surroundings and receives little attention, is unlikely to mimic. Mimicry is a way of identifying with and communicating with the person or persons to whom a parrot is closest. If it is frightened or lonely or unable to form a close bond with anyone, it is not very likely to talk.

- Talking ability varies in individuals and in species. Whereas some macaws are repeating their first words before they are weaned, few greys mimic well or mimic at all before they are one year old. This is interesting, because macaws seldom acquire an extensive vocabulary, whereas greys do.

- Certain sounds are difficult for parrots to repeat.

- Many new parrot owners have totally unrealistic expectations of their birds where mimicry is concerned. The simple fact is, the more time he or she spends with the bird, the more proficient it will become at mimicry. Someone who is out at work all day, should not expect their parrot to learn quickly, unless they have set sessions, morning and evening.

- Small parrots and many others respond better to a female voice or a child's voice because the higher pitch is more natural to them.
- It is dishonest of any seller to sell a bird stating that it will definitely learn to talk. So much depends on the relationship between the bird and owner and on the species.

The question which is asked over and over again is: Which are the best talking parrots? In other words, which species have the best potential for mimicry? Assuming that the parrot is obtained when young, that it is happy and well cared for, the answer would include the following species: grey parrot, double yellow-headed, yellow-fronted (yellow-crowned), yellow-naped and blue-fronted Amazons, quaker parrakeets, parrotlets, eclectus parrots, budgerigars and cockatiels. The potential for mimicry varies greatly among the Amazon species. The festive is another superb mimic—but is rarely available. In the U.S.A., the pet market is so large that, where Amazons are concerned, only the commercially viable species are bred in large numbers. Many of the others are destined to die out in aviculture there. In Europe, a wider range of species is available.

If you choose a species for its talking ability, remember that no parrot can reproduce the human voice with the accuracy of a

Amazons are extroverts and love to show off. This includes the author's yellow-front.

135

grey parrot. Many can speak in different human voices that are clearly recognisable. Other parrots cannot do that—or, if they can, they are exceptional. As an example, when Linda Greeson's grey parrot calls out "Come on in!" in response to a knock on the door, her friends enter because they believe it is her responding. But when her quaker parrakeet calls the same greeting, although they can understand the words, they do not enter. The tone of voice is obviously a parrot's! (Greeson, 1996.)

Linda Greeson commented: "Talking ability does vary with the individual. Many of the babies I raise are talking quite clearly before they are weaned. Most of the species are developing a rapidly increasing vocabulary by the time they are one year old. It is a rare one that does not talk at all, and most progress to phrases and short sentences within a short time."

The ability of the grey to faithfully reproduce individuals' voices is counteracted by the shyer temperament. Amazons, for example, are extroverts who love to show off. Greys are most likely to speak when they are not the centre of attention—or even when you are in another room. However, few parrots will speak when people crowd round them, anticipating their every word. In this case, they will be more interested in looking at the people. If you want to show off your parrot's abilities when you have friends in your home, the best way is to sit down, talk among yourselves and pay no attention to the parrot. He will then talk as a means of attracting your attention.

Individuals of countless species not mentioned above have made superb mimics. One generally finds that such birds have a very close bond with their owner. This means that they spend a lot of time together. This is really the key to teaching birds to talk.

There are two "personal" ways of teaching: giving a parrot actual lessons or repeating a phrase every time one passes by. In Pennsylvania, Dianne Albright has a highly talented celestial (Pacific) parrotlet (*Forpus coelestis*) who started to talk when he was two and a half months old. He had a vocabulary of 30 words by the time he was three and a half months. According to the Molendas in California, most parrotlets start to talk when between six and 12 months old. Dianne Albright described to me the method she used to teach him:

"Every day after breakfast Peppers and I have 'school.' He sits on his table-top perch and waits for me to talk to him. We started with 'Watcha doing' which he picked up from my pair of caiques. Soon he was saying everything the caiques said, including 'Gimme kiss,' followed by kissing sounds. Our school sessions last for ten to 15 minutes, as long as he pays attention. We have a similar session in the evening, repeating the phrases, and adding a new one when he has memorised another. I also repeat the phrases when I walk by him during the day.

"Peppers continues to learn and has not forgotten anything. He seems to pick up sounds on his own. He tries to imitate just about anything he hears from the computer printing, telephone ringing, water running, to adhesive tape being pulled from the roll. He is very attentive. He watches my mouth with every word I say during our sessions. It is not unusual for me to hold his attention for 20 minutes or more at a time. I think that it is his attentiveness and the daily repetition that has contributed to his extensive vocabulary."

It is difficult to say whether the parrotlet was exceptional—or his owner was. I suspect the latter. Dianne Albright is a caring and perceptive owner, the type to whom parrots respond very favourably.

There is another method of teaching to talk—using an electronic device! I believe it is available only in the U.S.A. to date. With this digital device, a parrot owner records his or her voice. This is played back at intervals during an eight-hour period. The period can be adjusted to give breaks of from five to 100 minutes and the training sessions can last from one to 20 minutes. (Global Engineering, PO Box 559, W. Lynn, Ma 01905). There are also speech-training videos which feature parrots talking.

As learning to talk is so greatly influenced by the parrot's relationship with its owner, my guess is that at least some birds would learn by listening to a recording of his or her voice. When a training video is used that features someone else's voice, I would expect the success rate to be low.

Mattie Sue Athan described the disappointment of a couple who bought a young grey parrot because they were so intent on teaching one to talk. Within a short time they were given a pair of cockatiels, a quaker parrakeet and a Goffin's cockatoo. Two years later none of the birds spoke more than one or two words. They were so disappointed that they were considering selling them all. She was asked to advise them. She pointed out that, after the grey, the other four birds were acquired before the grey started to talk. The cockatoo needed a lot of attention so she was handled more than the Grey. As a result, the Grey made sounds which resembled those of the Goffin's—"seeking to attract the attention given to the cockatoo." The advice given was to spend more time playing with the grey and inventing games which involved calling out to a hidden friend. As the Goffin's had the tallest cage, it perceived itself as dominant. "The African grey's previously normal behavioural development as only (dominant) bird was thwarted and the baby parrot had to re-evaluate its lower status. Under many circumstances, birds in lower situations make no noise at all, possibly because of concerns about safety." (Athan, 1997.)

Peppers the parrotlet was repeating 30 words by three and a half months old.

The couple bought a cage like the cockatoo's for the grey. They situated his perches so that if he wished, he could always be looking down on the cockatoo and the quaker. The cockatoo did not notice the change—but the quaker did and his perch also had to be raised. The cockatiels were given away, so that each of the three birds then received more attention. It was suggested that all the birds would benefit from full-spectrum fluorescent lighting, as the lighting in the room was indirect. When the full-spectrum lighting was installed, the parrots immediately became more active and more vocal.

Another improvement was to cover the birds at night. Before uncovering them next morning, each bird was given a little low-fat cheese. For the next 15 minutes or so they called to the parrots, asking if they were ready for breakfast. Soon the birds were peeping out from under the covers and vocalising for attention.

Within six months the grey had added a dozen words to his vocabulary, gave kisses and called the dog. Clearly, the grey had felt neglected. Improving his quality of life resulted in a bird who was starting to enjoy life and to vocalise in his owner's language.

I believe that the ability to mimic should be put to some practical use. Teach your parrot your telephone number. If he ever escapes, this could be the means by which he is reunited to you.

Do parrots understand what they say?

Some owners believe that their parrots understand everything. Others believe that they are only mimics. The truth lies somewhere in between and is partly dependent on how a parrot is taught to mimic. If you taught a child a nursery rhyme without explaining what the words mean, it would be repeating the rhyme "parrot fashion." How could it understand all the words unless you explained them? The same is true of parrots. If you use words only in the correct context, the parrot will quickly associate words with either objects or actions. If you say "apple" in a positive way before you give a parrot a piece of apple, and point at the fruit, he can learn to ask for "apple" when he wants a piece. If you say "water" whenever you put fresh water into the cage, he will associate the word with the fresh water; again, he could ask for it if the water container was empty. But if you teach him to say "I can talk. Can you fly?" he cannot possibly know what that means.

The most common use of association is saying: "Bye, bye" before you leave the house. It will not be long before your parrot says "Bye, bye" as soon as you make preparations to go out. When you put on your coat, this is a clear signal. Many owners who cover their parrot's cage at night say "Good morning!" when they uncover the cage. They find that most parrots say "Good morning!" only at that time. If you can hear your parrot practising the

139

words, do not repeat them during the day if you want to hear them only when you uncover the cage.

You will hear most parrots mumbling a phrase in an indistinct way, as though practising, before they perfect the words. However, some very clever mimics learn so quickly that this stage is omitted. Try to use a positive and lively tone of voice when teaching, as this will catch your bird's attention.

Mimicking various sounds

Some owners are driven crazy by their parrot's ability to reproduce sounds so accurately that they do not know whether it is the imitation or the real thing. The telephone gives the most problems in this respect! This is especially the case if one is in another room. Good mimics will copy any sound that they hear often—a dog barking, a cat meowing, or a squeaky door. If you have a grey who is an excellent mimic, don't buy a Moluccan cockatoo! One shrieking cockatoo is more than enough!

Copying actions

Some parrots are so clever and observant that they will copy actions, as well as sounds. One of my favourite descriptions of this talent was related by W. T. Greene, writing in the 1880s. A slender-billed cockatoo (long-billed corella) excelled in its version of clipping the laurel trees, after watching a gardener perform this task. "When he came in, we had the whole performance of clipping laurels gone through exactly, giving his head a little jerk with each snap of the shears—his beak was of course supposed to be those implements—and the sound was exact."

Many parrot owners fail to realise just how observant their birds are. They pick up cues from your behaviour and often know what you will do next. They are very aware of everything that is going on around them and enjoy the stimulus of different sights and sounds. They will become bored by always being in the same position and will enjoy the stimulus of being moved around the house where they can copy new sounds and even actions.

Chapter 14

Plumage care

It always makes me feel sad to see a parrot whose plumage has been neglected—not by the bird but by the owner. One can see with the briefest glance: the feathers look dry and lustreless. Many people fail to understand that water on a parrot's plumage is as important for its welfare as is good nutrition and a loving attitude. Can you imagine what it would be like never to have a bath or shower? Then try to imagine how it would feel if you could never wash your hair. It would soon look dirty and lifeless. In fact, it is much worse for a parrot never to be soaked to the skin. Parrots have powder down feathers which grow continuously. These disintegrate to produce a powder which the parrot uses to clean its plumage. The powder disperses when the bird enjoys a rain shower, holding open its wings to ensure that the rain reaches all areas of its plumage. If it did not get soaked on occasions, the build up of powder would be so enormous that when it shakes its feathers a big cloud of dust would be given off. This is precisely what happens to many pet birds whose owners fail to spray them or give them a bath. No wonder so many owners suffer feather allergies! When a shaft of sunlight strikes the air near a parrot kept indoors, even a well-showered parrot, it is possible to see that the air is filled with these dust particles. Some species give off more dust than others. The white cockatoos probably give off most. Greys are not far behind.

The dust is perfectly natural—but the build-up is not. Parrots need to be sprayed for the following reasons:

1. Humidity is needed to maintain the plumage in good condition.

2. As already stated, water is necessary to disperse feather dust.

3. Bathing is an exuberant activity which is enjoyed to the full.
4. Bathing helps to loosen particles of shed skin and feather debris.
5. Bathing stimulates constant preening which helps to maintain the feathers in good condition.

Most parrot cages have very small water containers in which bathing is impossible. However, if you see your parrot ducking his head in the water you should know that this is a hint that he wants a bath. There are three basic ways of ensuring that your parrot's plumage receives enough water. The method I have always used is simply spraying with a plant mister. The nozzle can be adjusted to produce a very fine spray. I use lukewarm water which comes out cold. The temperature of the water falls as it leaves the sprayer. It is not necessary to add any commercial product to the water. Indeed, as not all parrot species have the same requirements, such preparations may not be suitable for all species.

With young birds give a light misting at first, or even just mist the area around the parrot. Gradually increase the quantity of water on the plumage. Respect the fear of an older bird which has perhaps never been sprayed before by using the finest possible spray and giving him a very light shower. At first do this by spraying above him so that the droplets fall down over his plumage. Some parrots relish being sprayed from the time they are weaned. Others are much more cautious at first but grow to like it. For birds which are nervous of strange objects, it is a good idea to leave the sprayer within sight of the cage, before actually using it.

My Amazon will open her wings in anticipation at the sight of the mister. If the cage is small and

A plant mister is ideal for spraying a parrot.

142

has a removable base, you can place it in the sink while spraying. The second method is preferred by some birds but is practical only in a sizeable cage. A leaf of lettuce or spinach in a shallow container may encourage the parrot to start to bathe.

Thirdly, some owners take their parrot in the shower with them. I have never done this and would be quite concerned about the temperature of the water. It should not be too hot. Parrots can quickly become overheated.

What happens next? Assuming that the bird is in ordinary room temperature, it can be left to dry naturally. Wet plumage stimulates a parrot to preen itself vigorously, thereby ridding the plumage of flakes of dry skin and loose feathers. I also believe that it is good for the feet to be soaking wet on occasions. The new parrot owner may be alarmed at the apparent change of colour in the wet plumage of, for example, an Amazon parrot but, of course, this reverts to normal when dry. Then the beneficial effect of the shower can be seen, for the plumage of most species has a glossier appearance. It also smells nice.

Some people use a hair-dryer to dry their birds after a shower. Care is needed here. Again, the bird could quickly become overheated. Also, electrical appliances and parrots are not a good combination! Only in exceptional circumstances when it is necessary for the bird to become dry very quickly would a hair-dryer be recommended.

How often should a parrot be sprayed or have a bath? I would suggest a minimum of twice weekly and daily if this pleases your parrot. Lories, for example, will bathe almost every day, given the opportunity. The morning is the best time as it is not desirable for a bird to roost with damp plumage.

Many parrots live in centrally heated rooms where the atmosphere is extremely dry. Few of the parrots commonly kept as companion birds live in a dry atmosphere.

Greys, macaws and most Amazons, for example, come from areas of high humidity; cockatiels come from a more arid environment. It is common to see the former parrots which are kept indoors, with dry, dull plumage. Cockatiels, on the other hand, seldom have such an appearance. Obviously heating is necessary in cold climates—so what can be done to make the atmosphere less hostile to a parrot? The answer is to install a humidifier. There are several different types, not all of which are compatible with parrots. One which produces a warm mist is most likely to be suitable. It is important to clean and disinfect the humidifier on a regular basis. Note that if the room became too damp, it could be equally harmful as being too dry because moulds and spores thrive in such an environment.

The moult

During the course of one year parrots replace most of their feathers, although young birds have only a partial moult on the first occasion. In some species the moult is quite protracted and confined to certain areas of the body—first the head, perhaps, then the flight feathers. The complete moult may take three months or more. Flight feathers are shed over a long period, so that the bird is not rendered flightless. If you are ever presented with a bird that lacks flight or tail feathers and you are told that it is moulting, don't believe it! This is a totally unnatural state caused by feather plucking, PBFD (see Chapter 18) or polyoma virus. In other words, a very untruthful person is trying to sell you a sick bird. During the moult it would be unusual for the wing or the tail to be missing more than two or three feathers at the same time.

Feathers are made of protein. Additional protein during the moult is therefore beneficial. Cooked chicken is a good way to provide this and one that will be greatly enjoyed by most parrots. It is also a good idea to provide a vitamin and mineral supplement at this time—but don't overdo it. Follow the instructions. More is not better. An excess could be harmful!

Feather abnormalities

If you see any abnormalities in the new feathers you might need to consult an avian vet, depending on how severe these are. Stress lines, that is, dark lines crossing the feather, are an indication of stress or dietary deficiency when the feathers were being formed. This might have been a temporary condition which has since been corrected. Feathers which do not open because the quill is retained are an indication either of an excessively dry

144

environment or a vitamin deficiency. This is sometimes seen in the tail feathers of macaws.

Yellow feathers in green plumage or white feathers in blue or grey plumage may indicate a lysine deficiency. Abnormally brightly coloured feathers, such as red in a green or grey bird, might indicate liver damage. Other abnormalities, such as feathers which break easily, fall out before completing their growth or contain blood in the quill, are usually an indication of serious disease. The exception is when a bird falls or damages its tail feathers; this could result in blood in the quill.

Continuous moulting
If your parrot is in an almost continuous state of moult, something is wrong with the environment. It is said that excessive light can cause this.

A "shock" moult
Parrots can respond to a severe shock by moulting their flight feathers simultaneously.

Blood loss from blood quills
Occasionally a growing feather is damaged, causing loss of blood from the feather shaft. When the feather is fully grown, there is no longer a blood supply to the feather. Loss of blood from a broken wing or tail feather can be severe. If the bleeding does not stop after a couple of minutes, or after the application of flour, the broken feather should be pulled out. This is done by grasping it at the base, at the same time putting pressure on the area surrounding the base of the feather under the skin, to prevent the skin being torn. In a large bird such as a macaw, needle-nosed pliers can be used to pull the feather. Removal of the feather causes the artery to collapse, thus the bleeding ceases. If you can see no injury to a bird which is bleeding, a broken blood feather is the most likely explanation. It is worth noting that birds have a higher tolerance to blood loss than do mammals. Over the years I have seen a large pool of blood in cage or aviary on numerous occasions but only on one of these did the bird need to be given fluids. It was a lory. In lories and fig parrots blood clotting does not occur so quickly; it may be necessary to give Vitamin K.

Chapter 15

The feather plucker

Feather plucking is the most common problem among parrots of certain species, especially greys. It is also one of the most difficult to cure. If steps are taken to solve the problem immediately, there is a good chance the bird will be cured. Once plucking becomes a habit, that habit will be hard to break. Feather plucking is when a parrot pulls out its feathers, usually leaving the shaft still in the skin with the larger feathers, such as flights and tail. With the smaller feathers, such as those of the breast, the whole feather is usually removed. When a bird bites off part of the feather, so it has a ragged appearance, I would call this feather picking. However, for the purposes of cause and treatment, they are the same.

A bird usually commences feather plucking of its own plumage on the breast. (It is most likely to pluck its companion on the head.) The first step is to try to discover why feather-plucking is occurring. The causes can be placed in two main categories: psychological problems and ill health.

When presented with a feather-plucked parrot, a competent avian vet will carry out the following: a complete physical examination, faecal analysis, bacterial cultures, blood analysis and, where possible, viral tests. These will rule out or confirm psittacine beak and feather disease (PBFD) as the cause. As feather loss occurs in PBFD, it could be confused with feather-plucking. Polyoma virus also causes feather loss (see Chapter 18). Liver disease can also result in a bird plucking itself. A skin irritation might be to blame, especially in a parrot which is not regularly sprayed. Other possible causes in the ill health category are infestation of *Giardia* (a protozoal parasite) and bacterial infection of the skin or feather follicles. However, a bacterial infection could occur as the result of consistent plucking.

Feather plucking is more common in some species than in others. It is very common in greys. It is frequently seen in eclectus, cockatoos and the larger macaws. All these species have a sensitive temperament. They are easily stressed. In my opinion, feather plucking is more often caused by psychological problems, which is why it is so common in these species. It is not frequently seen in Amazons which, in my opinion, are not as easily stressed as greys and cockatoos.

Chris Hall, an avian vet in London, sees between eight and 12 feather plucking parrots every week, or about 500 cases every year. This number indicates the seriousness of the problem. He states: "Treatment is usually a combination of environmental enrichment, training, dietary change and the use of drugs—usually mood modifiers, hormones or endorphin blockers." (Hall, 1997.)

Some parrots apparently pluck themselves as a reaction to something to which they are allergic. One Grey stopped plucking after her owner changed to bottled water when bathing her. Apparently the minerals in the water softener irritated her skin. Sally Blanchard, editor of *The Pet Bird Report*, believes that some cases of feather plucking may be directly related to the bird's sensitivity to the cleaning agents used in the home. (See also Chapter 16.)

Where psychological causes are suspected, one has to evaluate every case. The owner should think hard about any changes which have been made in the bird's environment before plucking commenced. He or she should write down everything they can think of, no matter how insignificant it may appear. Changing the position of the cage, providing a new cage, introducing a new bird to the household or the loss of someone to whom the bird was greatly attached, are the type of situations which could trigger feather plucking. Or perhaps the parrot has spent a few days in someone else's house during the owner's absence. Anything which causes a parrot to feel insecure might be the cause.

Letters seeking advice on the problem are often received—but they almost never contain enough information. The owner usually describes the diet—and little else. Yet the diet is rarely to blame. One lady wrote to me about her hybrid macaw; she also kept another macaw. She was at a loss to know why the hybrid, which was believed to be about 18 months old, was plucking herself. One can only hazard a guess, given the bare details. Perhaps the hybrid macaw was older than suggested and in breeding condition (even only one year older). Frustration at being unable to breed yet housed in close proximity to a male, could have caused her to

Large pine cones were provided to distract this cockatoo from plucking himself.

pluck her breast feathers. Did the two macaws come out of the cage at the same time? If so, was the male, who was older, making sexual advances to the female who is not old enough to respond? This could also stress her. It was stated that she was more nervous so my guess would be that plucking was psychological in origin.

Course of action

When a parrot starts to pluck itself it seems that many owners assume that the bird must have lice or mites. This is very rarely the cause. They spray the parrot with a mite spray for birds. If this has no effect they may not make any further effort. Unless an isolated incident caused the bird to pluck itself out of stress, parrots seldom cease to pluck themselves until the cause of the problem is removed. In many cases the cause is never known and the bird is denuded for life—a sad spectacle. The owner may then lose interest in the bird completely. He cannot even give it away. Through no fault of its own, the unfortunate bird is condemned to a miserable life.

I would implore anyone whose bird starts to pluck itself to seek help immediately. When he or she does so it is quite possible that a different answer will be given at every turn. This is very discouraging—but there is no magic cure. The owner must work hard to try to get to the root of the problem.

Jealousy

A very common cause is jealousy. A parrot which has never plucked a feather in its life could be naked within a few days. If, for example, it has always been the only pet bird, doted on by its owner, and another bird was introduced to the household, this would be a psychological trauma of the first degree. Maggie Wright's grey had her constant attention, because she worked from home. Then a young grey was rescued. She described how her first bird, Merlin, was so jealous she started plucking. She pulled a red tail feather out right in front of her. Her owner took it from her (a mistake—she should have ignored her) and Merlin pulled out another. She took the second from her, and she pulled out a third. (Wright, 1997.)

Fear

The cause of plucking might be obvious to an experienced parrot keeper. I recall an incident with a young male eclectus in the breeding centre at Palmitos Park. He was one of about 20 young males kept in a large aviary. When he plucked his flight and tail feathers I guessed at once the reason. He was threatened in that situation. He did not like being among so many birds. He was the only one who reacted in this way. As it was impossible to find aviary space for a single bird, I put him in a cage and took him to my house. He received no special attention—only good food and frequent spraying. When he moulted the stumps of the flight and tail feathers and the new feathers appeared, he did not pluck them. Five or six months later he looked magnificent. Four pairs of eclectus were exported to a lady in Denmark, for her breeding aviaries, and he was among them. If she had seen him when I put his ring number on the export list (it took months to organise the paperwork) she would not have wanted him! Had he stayed in the large aviary he would probably have died of stress and misery. Birds react differently to the same situation.

What you can do

If your bird is plucking himself and you do not know why, I would suggest the following:

1. Think about it. You may need the sleuthing ability of Sherlock Holmes and the powers of observation and interpretation of Konrad Lorenz. But the answer may come to you.

2. Make sure your bird ALWAYS has something to chew on. It is difficult to keep up a continuous supply of branches. Circular cotton rope swings are excellent; they provide hours of chewing. If threads are hanging loose, cut them off as close to the frame as possible, to prevent your bird catching his nails in them. If you have the most destructive birds, such as cockatoos and large macaws, this will not be adequate. These birds need constant mental stimulation as well as, on a daily basis, branches, large pine cones and anything safe which can be destroyed, such as telephone books. Toys which contain various leather strips and pieces of hard wood may also be effective. I favour teaching macaws and cockatoos tricks; learning helps to prevent them from being bored.

3. If your bird is not lacking in mental stimulation and items for gnawing, consult an avian veterinarian and ask him to perform the usual tests. If you have any doubts about your bird's diet, ask the vet. However, this is not the time to change from a seed-based diet to a pelleted diet. A plucking bird does not need any extra stress factors in its life.

4. Make sure your bird is sprayed or showered at least twice a week. Daily is better if he enjoys it and you have the time.

5. Do not keep your parrot in a very dry environment or in the same room as a gas fire. Use a humidifier, if necessary.

Treatments

Some vets may use drugs, antihistamine in the case of an allergy, or hormones. They may be effective where they are the appropriate treatment. Alan Jones, an avian vet, suggested the administration of progestagens, such as megestrol acetate (Ovarid) at the rate of 5 mg/kg once a week for four weeks, then once a month. (This approximates to one quarter of a 5 mg tablet for a bird the size of a grey parrot. It could be given inside a favourite tid-bit.) Injectable agents such as Depo-proven or Delvosterone may also be used at 30 mg/kg to 40 mg/kg. He warned that these drugs may cause polydipsia or polyuria (too much urine), and lethargy or depression. Long-term usage is dangerous. These drugs may have short-term value in breaking the "itch/pick" cycle. (Jones, 1992.) However, I believe that drugs should be a last resort. First of all follow the example of Gloria James.

Green willow wood

Gloria James saw a "trembling, naked baby" grey in a pet shop. He did not utter a sound. He was such a contrast to her own beautiful grey that her heart went out to him. She bought him. She quarantined him for 30 days. It took months to win his trust. She would take her lunch to his room and eat in his presence, giving him fruits and vegetables which he had never had before. She made him toys from wood and leather. She cut up cardboard tubes into rings and knotted paper towels to the cage bars to keep him busy. He enjoyed them but continued to pluck. She then tried moving him into the living room with the other birds. This stressed him, increasing his plucking. He was moved back to another room. He began to talk and seemed happy and social, walked about and played with his toys. He was frequently misted. He was then moved again to join the other birds and this time adjusted to the move. But he was still plucking. Then a friend gave her some parrot toys she had made from chunks of green willow. He chewed and chewed and peeled off the bark. (Did the content of willow which apparently resembles aspirin have any influence?) Gloria James bought lengths of clean, uncut willow. These were sawn into little logs, 5 cm to 7.5 cm (2 in. to 3 in.) long, with a hole drilled through them. Untreated leather strips were threaded through the holes. As soon as they were destroyed they were replaced. More and more feathers appeared on his body. He did not remove them! His feather plucking was cured. Gloria James wrote: "We worked from the moment he came home with us to

151

improve his life and while all the improvements certainly made a difference, it appears the best thing was giving him so much chewing stimulation...little Alex is my heart. I can't imagine life without him. He brings such joy into my life." (James, 1997).

The collar

Some vets recommend the use of a collar to stop plucking. If a parrot is insecure or lacking in mental stimulation (just plain bored!) it is unlikely to make any difference. In most instances I do not agree with putting a collar on a bird. The quality of its life is greatly reduced. The feathers will grow back, if the collar is left on long enough. However, unless the root of the problem is determined, the plucking will recommence with the removal of the collar. If the bird has an injury or has had surgery a collar will prevent it from biting at the site of the injury. But the use of a collar for a feather-plucker is only a temporary solution and initially will cause the bird much stress. It is worse than pointless because it does not address the real problem. Other treatments, such as catching a bird on a daily basis to inject it, are likely to make the plucking worse. Stress levels must be kept down—not up.

Homoeopathic cures

Some vets are using homoeopathic cures for feather-plucking parrots. In Germany, for example, Dr. Rosina Sonnenschmidt has been doing so for several years. She has found that some parrots are cured with only three doses of a homoeopathic medicine. She uses the medicine in conjunction with her knowledge of parrot behaviour. For example, a Moluccan cockatoo was cured by giving it a large area, so that it did not have to be close to people, and with the use of homoeopathic medicine. However, this medicine can change a parrot's behaviour, so that it no longer is friendly toward its owner. Some diseases respond to a combination of traditional veterinary and alternative (homoeopathic) treatments. Her view was that many greys do not adapt well to the close presence of people and this results in feather plucking.

Chapter 16

Hazards about the home

When you bring a parrot into your home, it will be totally unfamiliar ground. If it is a young bird, just weaned perhaps, everything will look strange. This is especially the case for birds which have not been hand-reared in a home environment, or those from an aviary. What the owner must try to do is to look at his home with new eyes—the eyes of his parrot.

Look around the room and try to assess where hazards might lie. Could he fall behind a piece of furniture where you could not retrieve him without dismantling it? Check the fireplace for possible danger areas. Is there a small gap behind a gas or electric fire? Now look at the windows. Young parrots have no concept of what is glass, of course. But we can easily forget that. Whether or not your parrot is wing-clipped, he needs to know that window frames hold a clear substance that can knock him unconscious if he collides with it. If your bird can be readily handled, take him up to a window and move forward until his beak gently touches the pane. Do this in several different locations and do it a couple of times a day. If he is full-winged, only let him out of the cage when the curtains are closed until you are sure he has learned this lesson.

Doors and windows are generally at their most hazardous when they are open, whether or not your bird is wing-clipped. Even if he cannot fly, he can walk outdoors very quickly if the opportunity arises.

In the summer you might need to have a window open when your bird is out. Make a welded mesh screen on a wooden frame to fit over an open window; it can be painted to match the surrounding framework and held in position with wing nuts (on woodwork).

153

On the subject of doors, do not let your parrot get into the habit of perching on top of one. Reason one is that sooner or later he will start to gnaw the door, and reason two is that if the door is slammed shut in a wind he could be seriously injured or killed.

Other pets

Among the most dangerous items in many households are the furred and feathered occupants. Many parrots establish some kind of relationship with cats and dogs. Sometimes they hold the respect of the furred inhabitants on account of that dangerous weapon, the beak. Sometimes a friendly rapport may exist, especially if the bird and animal grew up together. But do not be lulled into a false sense of security by an apparently amicable relationship. One day a dog or cat may be teased beyond its endurance and react with a reflex action that could spell death to your bird.

Equally dangerous as the furred pets can be other feathered ones. The problem occurs when one parrot flies on top of the cage of another. That is viewed as trespassing—and the trespasser will get its toes nipped. This could result in serious bleeding or the loss of a toenail. The loss of blood can be difficult to stem. Make sure you always have on hand something to stem the flow of blood (see Chapter 14).

The living room

Parrots find cables irresistible for chewing purposes. If you have uncovered cables or appliances linked to extension cables, don't permit the parrot in the same room. It will find one sooner or later and could die as a result. Lampshades of the type which have a fringe of fine loops could also spell danger for a small bird. One cockatiel died, with its head trapped in a loop. New electric space heaters are potentially lethal. If you have a new one, use an extension lead to let it operate for an hour or so outside the house. When switched on for the first time many emit fumes which are lethal to birds. An American newspaper reported the sad story of a new space heater which was used to heat an indoor birdroom, 4.2 m (14 ft.) x 5 m (16 ft.). Within 20 minutes of turning on the heater the birds were distressed and falling off

154

This Jendaya conure, like most parrots, enjoys looking out of the window. Make sure the window is closed!

their perches. Within an hour all of the birds, more than 100, were dead. Apparently, the heating elements are often coated with paint so they do not rust. The coating burns and produces fumes.

Another hazard is carbon monoxide poisoning. If the fumes from a gas fire can kill people, they are many times more lethal to birds. A friend suffered the sad experience of watching four of his five birds die—an orange-winged Amazon, an Alexandrine parrakeet and a pair of peach-faced lovebirds. Strangely, a Meyer's parrot in the same room was completely unaffected. The following day the landlord had all the gas fires checked. One failed. In addition, the venting system was found to be inadequate. To monitor possible gas leakage, buy a carbon monoxide detector. The electrical plug-in models are recommended as there is a high rate of false alarms with the battery-operated detectors.

The kitchen

The highest risk room in your house is the kitchen. By now everyone who keeps birds should know that Teflon and other non-stick coated pans are potentially lethal. Apparently they don't—because every year birds die as a result of inhaling fumes from a burnt pan. These pans are safe if not allowed to exceed the temperature of 260°C—well in excess of normal cooking requirements. Small birds such as canaries are especially at risk, but any bird can die as a result of exposure to the fumes. If you burn a coated pan move the bird to another room instantly (or outdoors, if possible)—whether or not it is showing signs of distress. And open doors and windows to get rid of the fumes as quickly as possible.

The kitchen is often the most lived-in room in the house; therefore, many pet birds live there. But the constant change in temperature and humidity, as a result of cooking, do not make it the healthiest place for a bird to reside. Other risks include uncovered pans of water and a hot stove. Never, ever allow your bird to perch on the cooker. It cannot know that next time it lands there it may be red hot.

The bathroom

More than one pet parrot has drowned in the toilet. Insist that all members of the household close the lid of the toilet after use, and shut the door.

Lead and zinc poisoning

This is probably one of the most common forms of accidental death. It must also be one of the most heart-breaking for the owner. A number of items found about the house contain lead, zinc or other heavy metal. Examples are fruit juice cartons lined with silver paper, lead pencils, mirror-backing (contains mercury), curtain weights, metal key rings, some brass items (brass contains zinc) and old paintwork which may contain lead or even zinc.

You will know soon after if your bird has ingested part of any such item. It will drink much more than normal, there will of course be excessive urine (the white part) in droppings, and it may have convulsions or vomit. Its life will depend on the speed at which you consult a veterinarian. It will need fluids, Vitamin B1 and calcium EDTA which binds the metal and removes it from the bird's system. If treatment is commenced rapidly, recovery can be total. More insidious is the type of poison that builds up from a bird taking small quantities of perhaps lead or zinc from the powder-coating of its cage. Galvanised food dishes should not be given to destructive birds. Hangers for toys and chains should be made from stainless steel.

Cages which are constructed from rolls of welded mesh which have been badly galvanised must be carefully treated before use. There could be sharp or loose pieces of galvanising so the cage must be brushed with a wire brush before use, washed in vinegar, then washed again with a pressure washer. Even this may not be enough to remove jagged pieces of galvanising. The only answer is to have the cage powder coated. This is a process whereby paint in powder form is mixed with a resin and applied with a spray gun. It produces an exceptionally hard finish. Ensure that the paint used does not contain zinc.

One vet described how a lorikeet was diagnosed with metal particles in the ventriculus (gizzard). It was very sick but responded to therapy of chelation and psyllium. The source of the metal could not be found in the environment. The bird was confined to its cage but again showed signs of metal toxicity— polyuria (increased urine), loss of appetite and increased periods of sleeping. The cage and food were then scrutinised. A magnet was dropped into the food, and it was found to contain metal particles! X-rays were taken from the ground food mix, revealing further metal particles. (Bond and Muser, 1997.)

Although an x-ray will normally detect metal in a bird's organs, in some cases of slow chronic zinc poisoning, the amount of metal in the intestines is so small that it does not show up on x-ray.

Poisonous plants

Many house plants are poisonous to birds. If in doubt, keep the plants in a room to which your parrot does not have access. Plant material in another form can also be toxic—pot pourri. It is one of the hazards which are not widely known.

Mention must be made of cigarette smoke. Birds exposed to this over a long period may suffer adverse effects. It has been known for a century that small birds are very sensitive to fumes. That is why canaries were taken down mines to act as gas detectors.

Fumes from household cleaners can also kill—with speed. Remember that birds have a very low tolerance to many

chemicals; they are metabolised more than 100 times faster than in humans. In one sad case, 13 birds in a room which had been treated with a carpet freshener began to cough, wheeze and twitch after a carpet which had been treated with this product was vacuumed. The birds were moved to another room—but all died within 24 hours (Holtby, 1997). This kind of tragedy does not bear thinking about—yet it could happen so easily with the use of chlorine, ammonia, bleach, solvents and kerosene. Anything which makes you cough is 100 times more irritating to your parrot. Do not use any aerosols, including air fresheners.

Let us all try to make our homes a safer place for pet birds. There is nothing worse than to lose one in a tragedy that could easily have been prevented.

Chapter 17

What to do if your bird escapes

There is nothing sadder than the loss of a beloved pet due to a moment's carelessness; a door or window is left open or the cage door is not properly secured when the cage is placed outdoors. The golden rule in the latter instance is always to place the door against a solid surface, such as a wall. Many more parrots are lost when the owner takes a full-winged tame bird outside on his shoulder. The owner naïvely believes that because the bond between him and his bird is so strong, the parrot will not fly off. What he fails to realise is that fleeing from danger is an instinctive reaction. If the bird is frightened by, for example, a large vehicle or a dog, it will take off.

Although many escapees are recaptured, the majority are never reunited with their owner. A lot depends on whether or not the species is nomadic. If it is, it is more likely to travel a long distance. Cockatiels, for example, are notoriously difficult to recapture because they fly such long distances and quickly become lost. Thirty or forty miles in a day would not be exceptional.

Luck certainly plays a part—but there are a number of steps you can take to maximise the possibility of recovering an escaped bird. These include taking certain measures in advance, such as carefully recording all the ring numbers or microchip numbers of your birds. This is one of the few methods by which you can establish ownership. If you have had your bird DNA sexed using the blood technique, the company which carried out the sexing may store the sample free of charge. Comparing a blood sample with the one stored is another positive form of identification if your bird escapes or is stolen.

Notify relevant organisations

It is important to notify all relevant organisations: the police, animal charities such as the RSPCA in the U.K., and local animal rescue centres. Cast the net wide; do not only inform your nearest organisations but those in a radius of 40 miles or so, if you really want to recover your pet. You can also place cards in newsagents' shops or advertise in local newspapers. You have a better chance of recovering your parrot if you state that a cash reward is offered. Many people will go out and buy a cage if they find a bird—almost certainly a cage which is far too small because good cages are expensive. The philosophy would be: why spend a lot of money on something that is free? Therefore the size of your reward should be larger than the cost of the cage.

In the U.K., the weekly magazine *Cage and Aviary Birds* runs a free service in listing escaped (or stolen) birds. It is also worth contacting a local ornithological society. The members are more likely to notice and record an exotic bird than the ordinary public. Also contact local cage bird societies. Escaped birds are often attracted to aviaries or the calls of other birds.

Local media

Perhaps the most effective way of publicising an escape is in the local press or media. It is a good idea to telephone the news desk of the local paper or, better still, send a short story with a photograph of the escaped bird. However, be aware that to most members of the public one parrot is very much like another. Don't become too excited when your telephone rings. Ask the caller a couple of simple questions that hopefully will establish whether the bird they have seen or caught is the same species as yours. If it is, mention an identifying feature, if there is one, such as a ring (band), or perhaps a missing nail.

Catching an escapee

If your bird has been sighted but not caught, go to the place with his cage and some favourite items of food. If you have another bird with which the escapee is friendly, take him as well. If your bird is not tame enough to come down to you, place the cage as high as you can within sight of his perching place and attach a long string to the door, weighted by a brick on the ground. Test the way the string is attached to ensure that the door will close when the brick is removed. If he enters the cage, release the string and the door will close. If your bird comes fairly close, resist the temptation to grab at him or to try to net him. If you do this you will have only one chance as he will then become very suspicious. If you do make a grab he must be very close and you must be very quick. Very few people are quick enough. If he is tame, try to entice him to you so that you can tempt him with a tid-bit, then give the "Up!" command. When he is on your hand, close your finger on his foot; if you try to grab him with the other hand he will probably fly off.

Some escaped birds are enjoying themselves, perhaps feeding on fruits or berries. They have no intention of entering the cage. If they are not perched too high, hosing them down may be the answer. But make sure that the jet of water is not too violent. With very wet plumage, a parrot is unable to fly. In cold weather it could become chilled, so this step should be taken only in suitable conditions.

Remember that even the tamest bird may be afraid to fly down from a high point. Young birds or others that are unaccustomed to flying, might stay in that high place while a ladder is hoisted upwards. With very mobile birds it is usually a waste of time to attempt to reach them as they will fly when closely approached. (Think carefully before contacting the fire service; they can seldom afford the time or the manpower.)

Search the area
Some birds do not fly far, so it is worth making a thorough search of the area, continually calling out your bird's name. If he has a bell, take it with you and ring it. Do this for several days if necessary. Young birds, especially, may not fly far but sit quietly waiting to be found. Look around for landmarks, such as a high tree. A cockatoo or a macaw is most likely to make for such a location. If there is no sign of your bird after a few days, don't give up. Even in quite heavily populated areas, there may be numerous fruit trees or berry-bearing shrubs on which your bird could feed. Escaped parrots have been known to live free for months in suitable conditions.

Chapter 18

In sickness and in health

Unlike aviary birds, pet birds live in very close association with their owner. This means that the slightest change in the bird's behaviour, appetite, sleeping patterns, alertness or faeces should be noticed at once. Any change which cannot be explained easily should set alarm bells ringing in the owner's mind. Do not dismiss it. Think about it. If that change seems to suggest ill health, consult an avian vet immediately. One of the saddest aspects of a vet's work must be in seeing so many sick birds which could have been saved if the owner had sought advice as soon as he or she noticed something was wrong. Only very observant and experienced bird keepers will notice a change in a bird before it is very sick. They may delay going to the vet's surgery for one, two or even three days, hoping the bird will improve. When they do, it is often too late. The fact is, birds seldom recover spontaneously from whatever ailed them. In some cases, sadly, there is nothing that a vet can do; the bird might have damaged kidneys or liver, or a cancerous growth. But in many other instances treatment will effect a cure. You owe it to your bird to do everything possible to make that cure.

Start when your bird is in the best of health—in fact the day you buy him. Take out annual veterinary insurance. Veterinary care is never cheap. How would you feel if your bird needed expensive treatment but you could not afford to pay? The second step is to discover the nearest avian vet or one who is used to handling parrots. Do not wait until an emergency occurs. You might then rush to the nearest vet and find that he or she has no knowledge of treating birds. If you cannot find an avian vet, or cannot travel far, consult a vet who is prepared to take advice from an avian referral service.

Annual vet check

If you have an avian vet within reasonable travelling distance, you should consider the advantages of an annual veterinary check-up. It is often difficult to determine that a bird is sick until it is too late. But a simple blood test can reveal potentially fatal conditions which are not readily apparent. From a few drops of blood a complete blood count (CBC) is made. At the same time a culture can be made from the cloaca (vent) which will reveal the presence of harmful bacteria. It is important to find a vet who is used to making such tests; one who is not may not be familiar with normal findings in parrots. Unnecessary antibiotic treatment will do more harm than good. So will handling to take a blood sample by a vet who is not used to handling birds. The choice of vet is therefore an important consideration. If you do not know how to find an avian vet, consult a breeder in your area. Avian vets are listed in some avicultural and parrot magazines. In the U.K., *Bird Keeper* (a monthly magazine, published by IPC Magazines Ltd, King's Reach Tower, Stamford St, London SE1 9LS) and *Just Parrots* (published bi-monthly by Key Publications Ltd, 53 High St, Steyning, West Sussex, BN44 3RE) both list avian vets by county. In the U.S.A., *Bird Talk* (published monthly by Fancy Publications, PO Box 6050, Mission Viejo, CA 92690) carries advertisements under the heading of veterinary services and lists bird clubs by state. In Australia, *Australian Birdkeeper* (published bi-monthly, PO Box 6288, South Tweed Heads, NSW 2486) also lists avian vets.

What should you do if your bird becomes sick and you cannot take him to a vet until, perhaps, the following morning? First of all, make sure he is warm. The temperature in the vicinity of a sick bird should be at least 30°C (86°F); if the bird is small, a lovebird perhaps, it needs a higher temperature, about 32°C (90°F). A small bird can be placed in a hospital cage. A larger parrot should have the benefit of the heat from an infrared lamp. The ceramic (dull-emitter) kind can be purchased, with reflector and holder, from avicultural suppliers. These ceramic lamps (unlike the red glass ones available in hardware stores) are virtually indestructible. They are not cheap to buy, but they should last the bird's lifetime. The lamp is set up at one side of the bird's cage so that he can move away from the heat, if he desires. If you do not have an infrared lamp, it is difficult to provide the right kind of heat. Extra heat is vital because comparatively small animals and birds have a large surface area in comparison with their weight. They therefore lose heat very quickly. If they feel ill they do not want to eat, therefore they do not obtain the energy from food which would normally keep them warm. In response to this, a sick bird will fluff out its feathers for added insulation. A sick bird usually uses both its feet to support itself when sleeping; this results in further heat loss through the feet. A healthy bird tucks one foot into the plumage while sleeping, to prevent unnecessary heat loss.

It is very important that a sick bird does not become dehydrated so try to encourage him to drink and put some glucose in the water, if this is available. Many sick birds actually die of dehydration before the disease kills them. If a parrot does not eat for a few hours this will do him little harm but a small bird will deteriorate quickly without food. If he is tame enough to take something from a spoon, such as sweetened hand-feeding formula, this will be a great advantage. A recent development in veterinary medicine is the availability of products which assist the survival of a sick bird. For instance, in the U.K., the Birdcare Company markets Spark; this assists in rehydration and gives an energy boost. In Australia, Vetafarm produces Poly-Aid; this is also available in the U.K. No prescription is needed; they can be bought from many retailers. One of these or a similar product should always be on hand for an emergency, to add to the drinking water at the first sign of illness or, in the case of Poly-Aid, to feed into the crop.

On no account should you administer antibiotics. If you use the wrong type or overdose it you could kill your bird. The use of antibiotics will also invalidate the faecal analysis which the vet will request from a laboratory. Without this analysis, it is impossible to know which antibiotic will be the most effective, so days of precious time will be lost.

When a sick bird is taken to a vet, heat loss should be kept to a minimum. Heat the car, if necessary, and cover the cage with a blanket. Try to make an appointment with the vet so that you do not spend a long time in the waiting room. If it is warmer there, leave the bird in the vehicle until the vet can see your bird.

I would suggest taking your own towel for the vet to handle the bird; it should not be too large.

Below are listed some of the problems that could occur.

Beak abnormalities

A question which is often asked is whether it is normal for small pieces of the beak (keratin) to flake off. The answer is yes, to a degree; the beak is continually growing, as with our nails. However, if the flakiness appears excessive, a Vitamin A deficiency or a calcium deficiency might be the cause. If the beak is actually crumbling at the corners, suspect an infection of a *Candida* fungus. If the beak needs trimming, consult a vet. This is not only because he has the proper tools, and you do not, but because an overgrown beak might be indicative of a liver problem.

Hypocalcaemia

Low blood-calcium levels cause seizures; for an unknown reason, they are very common in grey parrots. This is why owners of greys are advised to ensure that a calcium supplement is given (but NOT in excess). If your bird is having seizures consult an avian vet immediately. There are two reasons for treating this as urgent. One is that the next seizure may be the last; the other is the difficulty in diagnosis. This consists of taking a drop of blood for testing. However, blood-calcium levels fluctuate. If testing is deferred for a few days, the level could be back to normal.

There is a belief that Vitamin A deficiency might be involved, so an affected bird's diet should also be supplemented with Vitamin A, under veterinary instruction. A vet can give a calcium injection or prescribe a calcium supplement.

Veterinary treatment

Many parrots respond very badly to being left for more than a few hours in a veterinary clinic. Just when they most need the love and care of their owner, they are abandoned in an unfamiliar environment. They must feel ignored and unloved; they are handled only for treatment. This might frighten them so much that they refuse to eat. Unless a parrot needs treatment more than once a day, it is advisable to return to the clinic with it as often as necessary, rather than leave it alone and afraid. One must also consider the risk of infection where sick birds are present. No matter how careful the attendants are, the risk from airborne disease is always present.

Parrots with outgoing personalities, such as certain Amazons and macaws, usually do not suffer so much at being "abandoned." But nervous, introverted birds, such as some greys, will simply stop eating. Perry Webb of South Africa, related what happened to his tame male eclectus parrot when it was sick and hospitalised. After one day the vet reported: "Your bird is sitting with its head under his wing; he is not eating and is not responding." The following evening the owner went to the clinic again, taking with him his own softfood mix. The vet said he was still refusing to eat. Mr. Webb filled a dish with the softfood and the eclectus began to pick slowly at the food. He ate three days' ration in one day and his condition immediately started to improve. Mr. Webb commented: "Seeing me may also have made a difference as he may have felt that we had abandoned him." (Webb, 1997.) The eclectus survived.

This story illustrates two important points. If a bird must be left with a vet, a supply of its normal food should be left, with strict instructions not to feed it anything else. A sudden change of diet is the last thing a sick bird needs! If Mr. Webb had not gone to the clinic, his eclectus would probably have died. Many vets are too busy to notice if a bird is not feeding well. Secondly, as Mr. Webb realised, what a parrot needs most when it is sick is the presence of its owner.

Handling and restraining

Many parrot owners have never been taught the correct method of holding a bird; as a result, if they need to do so in an emergency they will almost certainly be bitten. A towel should be placed over the parrot, the centre of the towel being over the head. If the cage is small, it may be easier to do this outside the cage. Grasp the parrot firmly through the towel, so that it cannot struggle. Feel for the beak and place thumb and forefinger just behind the mandibles; be careful to avoid putting pressure on the parrot's eyes and chest. By holding a bird in this way, you have immobilised the beak. If the bird is small you can do this with one hand. With a larger bird you can use your other hand to keep the towel firmly around the bird, while a second person cuts the nails or attends to a wound. Take care when you release the bird from the towel as he may turn round and bite you.

Every parrot owner should buy a suitable size catching net, even if their bird is tame. The net should have a padded rim. In an emergency it may be very useful.

Blood loss

If a bird is bleeding, the two most usual sites are from a broken blood feather (growing feather) (see Chapter 14, Blood loss) or from a broken toenail. If bleeding from a nail does not stop after a couple of minutes, an attempt to stem the flow must be made. Catch the bird, hold it in a towel and dip the nail into a cup of flour or cornflour. Keep the flour pressed against the nail until bleeding stops. Do not return him to the cage until two or three minutes more. If bleeding continues, any vet should be able to stop the blood loss with the use of a cauteriser.

Hypovitaminosis-A (Vitamin A deficiency)

This vitamin is necessary to maintain the membranes lining the eyes and throat in good order. Its deficiency results in abscesses and secondary infections, resulting in chronic respiratory disease from which many parrots die. Sometimes one sees a parrot which has a channel in the upper mandible below the nostrils, as a result of a constant discharge. Such unfortunate birds have been suffering for months and in many cases all they needed was supplementation with Vitamin A.

Nail trimming

The two most usual reasons for broken nails are extra long or curved nails which are trapped in something. This indicates that the nails need trimming. This is an easy procedure which could be carried out by a competent owner once he or she has been shown the correct method. However, some parrot owners do not wish to do this for fear of spoiling the relationship they have with their

Nails can be clipped using nail clippers for humans or special clippers for birds.

parrot. In this case consult a vet. Do be quite certain that the vet is used to handling parrots. Unfortunately, there are reports of vets totally mishandling nail-clipping. If you or anyone else cuts into the vein when clipping a nail, the blood will be seen at once. Do not continue or allow anyone else to continue. It indicates that the nail has been clipped too high up. Stop the bleeding and seek a more qualified person. In most parrots it is quite easy to see the vein, when the toe is held against the light. If the vein is cut, not only could loss of blood be serious but it will be painful for the parrot. Nails can be clipped using nail clippers for humans or, in the case of larger parrots, for animals, or special nail clippers for birds which are sold in some pet stores.

It is sometimes suggested that the nails of young parrots should be cut to stop them scratching their owner. This is not recommended; it will encourage nail growth, making regular clipping a necessity. Normally, this is so only with old birds. If the nails are sharp, file them. Young birds need nails of the correct length to help them perch and balance. Filing removes an insignificant part of the nail. Whichever method is used the bird should be held in a towel in the proper manner. This prevents him struggling. If he moved when you were cutting, you could cut too high up.

Polyoma virus

This virus is responsible for the deaths of many parrot chicks before they are independent. Small chicks look pale, suffer haemorrhaging and bruising and older chicks do not feather up properly. It is a papovavirus which results in Budgerigar fledgling disease in Budgerigars and more acute disease in larger parrots. It is also known to affect wild birds, such as sparrows. Tests available in the U.S.A. indicate that the disease is much more common than was previously thought. Although some adult birds develop an immunity which will eliminate the organism from the system, in most birds the immune system is damaged, which means they easily pick up disease. They may remain infected and be a source of infection by constantly shedding the virus. The polyoma vaccine from the United States is now available in Europe. Wise owners will have their birds vaccinated. And breeders will have their birds tested for polyoma.

Proventricular dilatation disease (PDD)

At the present time, this is the most serious disease to affect parrots. Also known as macaw wasting disease, it is not confined to these birds. Many species are affected and grey parrots appear to be especially susceptible. The proventriculus is the part of the stomach which produces gastric acid. The ventriculus, the adjoining section of the stomach, shoots food into the proventriculus, then it is passed backward and forward until it is broken down. In most affected birds, the proventriculus becomes greatly enlarged (dilated). Food is poorly digested and, in parrots which eat seed, undigested seed can be seen in the droppings. Although this is a major symptom in most birds, PDD is actually a disease of the nervous system which results in the inability of the proventriculus to function properly. Weight loss is usually the most obvious sign; other symptoms are weakness, polyuria (excessive amounts of urine in the faeces), listlessness and few droppings. At the time of writing, the best diagnosis was from a crop biopsy. Because the disease affects the nervous system, some birds appear unsteady or hold the head at an abnormal angle. However, all these symptoms are not necessarily indicative of PDD. Clinical findings are inconsistent and fungal or bacterial infections may complicate the laboratory findings. To date, no cure has been found for this disease. Most birds die within a few months, or a few weeks. Feeding them on processed foods (such as pellets) will slightly lengthen their life. However, the quality of life may be so poor that it is kinder to euthanise them. The virus which causes the disease is secreted in the faeces. Birds suspected of being infected should be isolated. Those kept indoors are the most susceptible.

Psittacine beak and feather disease (PBFD)

Affected birds which have moulted since contracting the disease have ragged plumage with missing feathers; the uninitiated often believe that it is caused by feather plucking. However, the feathers of the crown and, in cockatoos, those of the crest, will be affected, so this cannot be the case in single birds which cannot reach these areas. Examination of the feathers shows that they are fractured and may have several fault lines or stress marks. Feathers may be short or curled. Often there is blood in the quill. In white cockatoos the plumage has a dirty appearance. In many affected birds the beak is soft and deformed. Green birds may have patches of yellow in the plumage and blue birds (and Vasa parrots) show some white feathers. Ulcers may develop on the wingtips.

If you suspect that your bird has this disease, isolate it immediately from other birds. It may already be too late. The second step is to take feather samples to a vet for laboratory testing. This can confirm the disease; a negative result does not necessarily mean that the bird is free of the disease; it means it was not shedding the virus at the time. Another test is recommended. Do not take a suspected affected bird to your vet; if there are any birds in the surgery, the presence of your bird could put them at risk.

Sadly, most birds suffering from PBFD do not recover. They might linger for a couple of years but their quality of life is usually so poor that it is kinder to euthanise them. Partial recovery from acute PBFD occurs in a few species, such as the budgerigar, rainbow or Swainson's lorikeet and lovebirds. Cockatoos are usually the most badly affected.

This disease is caused by a circovirus which targets the feather follicle, thus an affected bird could appear normal until it moults. However, the liver may also be affected, in which case the bird may appear sick. According to Dr Garry Cross (1996): "The incubation period of PBFD may be as short as 21 days. How quickly the disease develops is dependent on the dose of the virus, the age of the bird, the stage of feather development, and absence of immunity."

Margaret Wissman (1996–97) warns that blood drawn for a PBFD test should be taken by venipuncture. If it is obtained by clipping a toenail and proves positive, the test must be repeated because virus contamination from skin or toenail could give a false-positive result. She emphasises that a young bird should not be euthanised based on one positive result. Some with normal plumage which test positive are able to fight the infection, and will become naturally immune to PBFD. When re-tested after 90 days, they will test negative. The virus has been cleared from the bloodstream and the bird has been naturally vaccinated.

Rings, removal of

Many breeders ring the young parrots they rear. This is especially important with the rarer species in order to aid identification and prevent in-breeding. The owner of a ringed parrot should note the ring number. It could be proof of ownership, if the bird was stolen or escaped. It is difficult to prove ownership of a parrot which does not have a ring, microchip or a distinctive feature, such as a missing nail.

There are occasions when removal of the ring is necessary; perhaps the incorrect size ring was fitted; as the bird grows the ring will bite into the flesh. The leg will swell and a parrot could lose its leg in a very painful manner if this was not detected in time. If a ringed parrot is noticed limping, the leg must be examined. If the ring is causing the problem, the bird should be taken to an avian vet immediately. Avian vets have experience of ring removal; other vets may not be aware of the correct method or have the necessary tool. One method is to use a high-speed dentist's drill which sprays water as it drills, to prevent the bird's leg from being burned by the heat of the drill. The ring is drilled through at two points so that the two halves of the ring drop off. If the leg is very swollen it may be advisable to reduce the swelling first. One method is to soak cotton wool in witch-hazel and hold it around the leg for a couple of minutes two or three times daily, until the swelling reduces. However, where the need for removal is urgent, this method could not be used.

Note that some vets routinely cut off rings (bands). Do not permit this, unless you have a good reason, in which case keep the ring or note down the information on it before it is removed. Many former pet birds are eventually used for breeding purposes. In this situation identification of individuals is important to prevent in-breeding. The information on the ring may allow you to identify the breeder.

Another fact to be aware of is that some vets (more usually in North America) routinely trim the beak of any parrot taken to them. On no account allow this unless the bird's beak is overgrown.

Seizures or fits
A common cause is low blood-calcium levels—see above under Hypocalcaemia. There are many other widely varying causes. An avian vet should be consulted immediately. Meanwhile, keep the bird warm and quiet.

Shock
A bird may go into shock if it has been traumatised. The problem here is that some happening which to the owner may seem inconsequential, severely disturbs the bird. As an example, a grey belonging to a friend crash-landed on the kitchen floor, which was not carpeted. Perhaps she bruised her underparts. She was visibly upset and was at once returned to her cage. For the next 48 hours she was very quiet and ate very little. As her owner saw what had happened, she knew that her grey was in shock. But if she had not witnessed the incident, she would doubtless have taken her to the vet—which would have traumatised her even

172

further. There is little that one can do to help birds which are in shock, except to keep them warm and quiet and ensure that they can drink as much as they want. For a large bird, like a grey, to go without food for two days is not life threatening, but in a small parrot it could be fatal. The use of an emergency food such as Poly-Aid would be vital.

Zoonotic diseases

These are diseases which can be transferred from birds to humans, such as *Chlamydiosis* (psittacosis). This is the only one in which this is likely to occur. The symptoms are flu-like, generally with a high temperature and fever. The use of the antibiotic tetracycline effects a rapid recovery in most humans (except perhaps in old people), provided that the disease is diagnosed early. The real danger is incorrect diagnosis. Anyone who has had contact with parrots, pigeons or other birds should mention this to a doctor and suggest that they might be suffering from chlamydiosis. Contact might be brief; for example, someone who visited a bird show and spent some time playing with a recently imported young grey parrot contracted the disease, apparently from the grey.

In the mid-1990s an absurd claim was made by Dutch researchers that parrots can cause lung cancer. Further studies revealed that this was totally incorrect.

Growing old

It is a myth that parrots can live to 80 or 90. Smaller species such as cockatiels can live to 30 or more and larger parrots rarely live beyond 50. Unfortunately, there is perhaps only one well documented study of the effects of old age. Many of the macaws hatched at Parrot Jungle, in Miami, over a period of 50 years (plus the original wild-caught birds) stayed in the collection and were studied by Dr. Susan Clubb. By the age of 35 to 40 years, most of them had cataracts. By 40 years, muscle wasting and weight loss was generally evident. Most had joint stiffness or arthritis; the facial skin was thin and some macaws had numerous skin blemishes. By 45 years many of the macaws showed signs of musculoskeletal degeneration, with twisted legs or toes and a stooping posture. Forty-five-year-old birds had a high incidence of neurological disease, stroke and blindness. Most of those which survived to 50 years were blind. The oldest macaw was euthanised when it was at least 57 years old. (Clubb, 1994.)

Many older parrots suffer from arthritis. As their grip is poor they are liable to fall off the perch in the night. The top perch should be lowered in order to reduce the fall. In very old birds feather loss will occur.

After I had had my Amazon 29 years, she was seen to retch early every morning. She was laparoscoped and x-rayed by an avian vet. He found that she had varicose veins at the entrance to the proventriculus. Perhaps this is the cause of the retching which is seen every morning for a few seconds. He also found a slightly raised level of liver enzymes (6.6); calcium and glucose levels were normal. The aorta was slightly enlarged. Signs of arthritis were apparent. The conclusion was that she was in reasonable condition; her age is unknown.

In loving memory
If a much-loved pet dies, do something positive in memory of him or her. Plant a tree in your garden or, on the anniversary of your loss, make a donation to the World Parrot Trust. In both cases, other birds will benefit.

Chapter 19

Questions from parrot owners

Relating some real-life situations where owners have sought help is a good way of demonstrating the type of problems which can arise. I have used all the relevant letters I received during the four months I was working on this book. It is significant that of the twelve letters, nine related to grey parrots. While this partly reflects the popularity of this species, it also indicates that many owners find these parrots difficult to understand and that behavioural problems are common.

Two grey parrots

Question: I have two African greys, both about eight years old. The old man who owned one died; she was pulling out her feathers. I have recently acquired her and placed her in a cage next to my own African grey. My bird feeds the new one and preens her feathers. They both seem very happy when this happens. My bird will not come out of his cage but the female goes to him. Would they be safe together if I bought a large cage? I am 71 years and my parrots are my life.

Answer: It certainly appears as though your two greys like each other. As they have already got to know each other, there is no reason why you should not obtain a large cage and put them together. If they do not seem compatible one could be returned to his original cage. It would be a mistake to try to keep them permanently in the cage of one or the other as parrots are very territorial. Introductions should always be made on neutral territory, that is, in a new cage. In any case, a standard size parrot cage is definitely not large enough for two birds.

Lovebirds, such as these peach-faced, may be suitable if they have been hand-reared.

A pair of lovebirds

Question: I am about to obtain a pair of young hand-reared love-birds. However, no two books seem to have the same opinion regarding their pet qualities. Some say they are noisy, others say they are quieter. One says that they make good pets, another that they are spiteful and unfriendly. I have been told that they will not be tame if there are two.

Answer: It is only comparatively recently that lovebirds have been hand-reared as pets. When only wild-caught or parent-reared young were available they were not recommended as pets because it was or is difficult or impossible to tame them, thus older books will not recommend lovebirds as pets. A single hand-reared young bird will make a good pet, if it is handled sympa-thetically. However, these birds mature quickly, thus if you have a pair you can expect them to lose interest in you before they are one year old. This is when they are likely to start breeding, if they are a true pair. Despite this, I believe that it is better to keep a pair. Incidentally, the personality of some females could be unfriendly when they mature. (In lovebirds, females are usually dominant over males.)

Hypocalcaemia?

Question: I have recently acquired an English-bred hand-reared grey who is fine except when he is tired. The wings jerk and the head jerks as though to some kind of nervous response. His wings also jerk when he is asleep. Why does this happen?

Answer: The symptoms you describe suggest to me that the problem is hypocalcaemia, or calcium deficiency. Unfortunately, this is a common problem in young greys because many breeders do not realise how much calcium this species needs. You were right to seek advice because the problem can be rectified if you act quickly. The first step is to ask a vet to give your grey an injection of calcium and Vitamin D. This will provide an immediate boost to the blood calcium level. Secondly, the vet should take a small amount of blood for a blood profile. This may confirm that hypocalcaemia is the problem. If left untreated, greys with hypocalcaemia will suffer from fits which eventually kill them. (See Chapter 18.) Also note that a deficiency of protein can result in tremors. While on the face of it sunflower seed is high in protein, if it does not contain all the necessary amino-acids, this limits the amount of protein which can be used. To ensure the good health of your grey over the long term, it would be advisable to replace seed with pellets or an extruded food. This will prevent further dietary deficiencies.

The name says it all!

Question: My problem lies with the strange and constantly changing behaviour of my African grey, O.J., who is 21 months old. My husband named him as he said that I would spoil him so much he would get away with murder! When I bought him he was about nine weeks old and I had to spoon-feed him. He was adorable—very quick to learn to perch and was always in my arms or on my shoulder. I placed a tree branch in a drum and put it next to the grey's cage, and that of my husband's sun conures. After a while, O.J. would climb to the top branch and would not come down. About three months ago he decided that he hated my husband. He screeched, flapped his wings and growled whenever my husband went near him—so he stayed away. A couple of weeks later he started treating me in the same way. A week after this behaviour started, the family arrived for a week with the grandchildren. It was probably upsetting for the birds with the kids running around. (Heaven alone knows what happened while I was out of the house during this time.) The day after they left more family arrived and while the second crowd were still there the third lot arrived. During this time both parrots spent most of the day in their cages. A few weeks later my husband bought me another grey. Due to lack of space we purchased a set of three stacking cages; each bird has a space 1 m (3 ft. 3 in.) square. On the advice of the breeder we took the tree away. O.J. loved his new cage. Suddenly he started to come to me again. Early morning I would take him upstairs and play with him, then put him back at breakfast time. However, once he went back in his cage he did not want to come out again. He growls, flaps his wings and tries to bite me if I try to get him out. I still feel hurt by his behaviour because if he is out of the cage and I enter the room, he goes like a bullet back into his cage.

Answer: The problems you are having with O.J. stem from the fact that he is totally confused. Grey parrots are very intelligent creatures who need guidance and rules from an early age. As in children, if they do not receive this, their behaviour becomes problematical in adolescence. You must establish some kind of routine so that your birds know what to expect on a daily basis. It is not good enough that they receive little attention for days on end when you have guests. Neither should they be kept permanently in a room where suddenly there are children creating a disturbance. No wonder their behaviour is erratic. Your birds need a) A quiet room where conditions are unchanged, when the children are staying in your house. b) Periods out of the cage at the same time each day. It does not matter if this is only for 20 minutes twice a day; they must know what to expect. c) Their own space. You are invading this by putting your hand in O.J.'s cage, except when you want him to come out. You should teach him the "Up!" command so that you are in control and only let him out when you take him out and have time to give him a lot of attention. In this way he will look forward to coming out, knowing that he will have your undivided attention. Be firm if he does something wrong, like biting. Say "No!" and immediately return him to his cage. If O.J. is a male he may be difficult at this time (approaching two years old) unless he receives guidance from you, calm but clear, on how he should behave.

On the subject of the stacking cages, I believe that such cages should NEVER be used for pet birds. Birds which live in the same area have an order of dominance, or a "pecking order." Height equals rank. To relegate the young grey to such a low position is unfair. Also, no pet bird should be at a level where it sees only the bottom half of people passing. The young one will be very aware of his low status and this could prevent him from learning to talk—but you may not be interested in this aspect. I would suggest that you have a base made so that the bottom and middle cages are elevated to the height of the middle and top cages. The young grey should take the top position and the conures the lower position. As they are a pair, rather than pets, they will be more concerned with each other's companionship than with status. O.J. should be moved to a place where his height is equal to that of the other grey, or to another room if he will have plenty of human companionship there.

Floor scratching

Question: I recently bought a 12-week-old hand-reared grey parrot. Sometimes he goes to the floor of the cage and scratches one of his feet backward and forward, again and again, kicking up the paper on the bottom of the cage. Why does he do this?

Answer: This is absolutely typical of grey parrots, also of some other African parrots. It can be annoying! It is usually done for attention, when the grey wants to come out. Provide toys in the cage to divert his attention from this habit that most greys grow out of after a few weeks.

Getting to know another person

Question: One month ago I bought a three-year-old grey parrot. When I first bought her she would talk for two or three hours in the evening. Now, when I am alone in the room with her she will talk and whistle. But as soon as my fiancée comes in she shuts up and does not utter another word. Also, she has not repeated one word which we have tried to teach her. All we hear is what she was taught in the past.

Answer: It is normal for greys not to talk in the presence of people they do not know very well. Also, they will not talk if they are being watched. As she gets to know your fiancée better it is likely that she will begin to talk in her presence, provided that your

179

fiancée is taking no notice of her. Unlike some parrots, such as Amazons, greys do not respond to people talking to them. They are more inclined to listen and watch. As you have only had her one month I think you are expecting a lot that she should already be repeating new sayings. Greys are quite nervous birds who often take a long time to settle down in new surroundings. The fact that she was talking so soon after you obtained her is good. Do not expect too much of her. She will repeat new words in due course. It is impossible to say when. Greys are individuals; their actions cannot be predicted.

Squawking for attention

Question: When I put my hand-reared African grey parrot back into her cage she squawks loudly for attention. How can I stop her doing this?

Answer: I suggest that you have her out at times when you can leave the room or go out as soon as you put her back in her cage. She is squawking for your attention but if you are not in the room she will probably cease to do this fairly quickly, realising that it is pointless. If it is not possible to follow this advice, you could try covering the cage with an old towel when you put her back. She will probably start to nibble at this in annoyance and this will keep her busy. Make sure she has a few toys in her cage to keep her occupied.

Maturing kakariki

Question: I am having problems with my kakariki. He is about six months old, a hand-reared male who, until about two weeks ago, was a very friendly and loving bird. His attitude towards me has changed totally. He is still very friendly towards my fiancé but if I am in the room when he is out of his cage, he constantly bites me. We have tried to stop him biting by putting him back in his cage but it makes no difference. I now leave the room before he comes out. I consulted a vet who told me I should take the bird to an animal psychologist.

Answer: Unfortunately, the vet seems to have little understanding of birds. What your kakariki needs is quite simple—a mate! Kakarikis mature at six months old—the age of your bird. I doubt

Kakarikis are aviary birds. They should not be closely confined as pets.

very much that the behaviour of yours will improve on a permanent basis. You have two options: to let him go to a breeder, or to buy a female for him and build an aviary. Kakarikis need a flight about 3.6 m (12 ft.) long. Incidentally, I think it is irresponsible of breeders to sell kakarikis as pets. These birds are very active and should not be closely confined. Also, as you have discovered, most of them do not make suitable pets when they mature.

Grey has ceased to talk

Question: My African grey parrot has stopped talking. How can I get him to start again?

Answer: There are several possible reasons. He might be sick. If he is eating less than normal, sleeping more and if his droppings are abnormally coloured, he is ill. You should consult a vet immediately. Another possibility is that he has had a shock or severe fright. Or something in your grey's surroundings or circumstances has changed, and this has upset him. It could be the addition of a new bird to the household, the absence of someone he is fond of, or even a new cage or location. Greys are very sensitive birds and even placing a new toy which he does not like inside his cage could cause this change.

Biting Amazon

Question: My nine-year-old yellow-fronted Amazon bites and butts me but adores my husband. I was advised that only I should feed her and that I should stop wearing perfume. This advice has not worked.

Answer: The key fact in your letter is that your Amazon adores your husband. She considers herself to be bonded to him and looks on you as a rival for his affections. Her apparent dislike of you is nothing personal. You just happen to be your husband's wife! This problem is quite common in parrots which form strong pair bonds. It will make little difference whether you or your husband feeds the Amazon. And wearing perfume has nothing to do with the situation. The main problem, provided that you can accept that the Amazon will not change her mind about you, is that you are allowing her to dominate you. You must break the behaviour pattern whereby she attacks and bites you whenever she feels like it. She must be confined to her cage except when your husband is spending time with her and then it would be advisable for you to be elsewhere. If you continue to let her attack you she will believe that she is at the top of the pecking order in your house and she will make your life a misery.

Grey's seed diet

Question: My African grey eats plenty of seed but very little fruit or vegetables. Are there enough vitamins in this diet?

Answer: No. Greys that eat only seed are unlikely to survive long as their diet is deficient in Vitamin A and in calcium. Without these vital components, grey parrots develop serious respiratory infections, including nasal discharges and hard lumps. They may also suffer from hypocalcaemia. It is vitally important that your grey learns to eat a better diet. I would suggest reducing the amount of seed offered. In the morning give a small amount with mixed fruits. A piece of banana can be offered in a separate container. If you fill the container with seed he will not be hungry and therefore will not try other foods. In late afternoon give a little more seed and perhaps a piece of corn or raw carrot. As pomegranates are available at the time of writing, I would suggest cutting this fruit and mixing some of the red seeds with the sunflower. This is one of the most popular and beneficial fruits you can offer. The season ends in December, but once your grey starts to take new items, he will be more adventurous in his diet.

I would also suggest that you add fruit to his toys so that when he is playing with them he finds a grape or a piece of orange, for example. Also offer small twigs with hawthorn berries. He may be a little nervous of them at first. When he is used to them and eating the berries, you can impale pieces of fruit on the twigs. Once he is eating fruit you can add a small amount of a powdered calcium supplement.

Avian nutritionists favour feeding grey parrots on extruded foods or pellets as these contain all the nutrients essential for good health. However, it is often difficult to convert greys to these diets as they will not eat them if sunflower seed is available.

Plucking grey

Question: One month ago we were given a three-year-old African grey. He has a few flight feathers and head feathers, but otherwise he is covered in down. The previous owners only ever fed him seed. We have improved his diet. He has a large cage which is left open; he climbs all over it and has plenty to play with. However, we cannot keep him in the kitchen where the family spends most time, because we keep birds of prey and have to carry them through and we do not want the parrot to feel under threat. He is in the living room and we leave the radio on when we are out. Some days he is really chatty. We have tried an anti-peck spray but this stressed him as we had to cover his eyes to avoid harming him. We would like to help him as he is very entertaining and seems to have a sense of humour. Can you suggest what we can do?

Answer: Curing a long-term feather plucker is never easy. I do feel your grey would benefit from being moved to the

A circular cotton rope swing provides hours of gnawing entertainment. The loose threads should be cut off.

183

kitchen where there is more human companionship. If the birds of prey are hooded when you carry them through, he may not be afraid. The extra activity will help to take his mind off feather plucking. However, if he does seem afraid, you will have to move him back to the living room. Make sure he always has plenty to chew on. Start with twigs, so that they do not frighten him, then progress to pieces of branches from poplar, willow, apple, pear, etc. Also provide a small circular cotton rope swing; they provide hours of chewing. An anti-peck spray will not be effective. Feather-plucking is normally either psychological or due to a health problem. It would be advisable to have him checked by an avian vet. A simple blood test or faecal analysis might reveal that there is something wrong with him which is causing him to pluck himself.

Chapter 20

Ambassadors who fly between both worlds

Through our birds, we can instill in others the importance of being at one with the natural world. We can use our close association with certain birds in our home to show how birds have an intelligent awareness that equals our own. They are therefore as deserving of respect as any human being—more so, some might say, since they are at one with their world. We are not.

We force our birds to live in an unnatural environment; our destruction of their habitat compels birds in the wild to adapt to man-made landscapes—or die out. Our own pet birds can help to re-establish the bond that should exist between nature and man. They can be ambassadors who fly between both worlds.

We can educate our children and our friends' children by showing them the intelligent, thinking actions of our parrots. We can explain that they have the same emotions as us, the same ability to think through problems and revise their behaviour accordingly. They have good cognitive abilities (are able to know and perceive many things).

They recognise individual people as readily as we do, just as they recognise individual members of their flock. Some species of birds which breed in immense colonies can recognise their own chicks among hundreds or thousands of others—just as we can identify our friends and acquaintances.

Except for the ability to create complicated objects which are of no use to other species (and are often extremely harmful), we are in no way superior to birds or other animals. When we learn this lesson, we will accept that man must not be allowed to dominate the universe.

Because birds live in the homes of so many of us, we can learn to communicate with them, and they with us. This is already happening in hundreds of thousands of homes. Pet birds must not exist solely to please their owners, but to demonstrate that real, intelligent communication between humans and other animals is possible.

Because parrots can mimic, they can learn some of our language. Because they are intelligent and highly social creatures, they can learn to communicate with us in our own language, to a limited degree. Alas, very very few humans have ever learned to communicate with animals in their language. Again, this shows how in some respects birds are superior to us.

They deserve our respect; they are not automatons; they are beings covered in feathers who learn, during their often short lives, how to use and perfect many skills. They also give immense pleasure to countless humans. Alas, comparatively few humans give joy to birds.

The most important legacy that any human can leave is not (unlike birds and animals) its genes in the form of another generation, but to sow the seeds of love, respect and understanding for the natural world in today's young people. Unless we do that, most of the world will become uninhabitable for the majority of its life forms.

Michael Reynolds, founder of The World Parrot Trust, coined the phrase: "If man can save the parrots, he can yet save himself." This is not a glib catch-phrase. It is the truth. The status of birds in the wild (more so than mammals because they are more readily observed), is an indicator of the health and viability of natural environments. This is especially true of parrots; being beautiful, even spectacular, conspicuous and widespread, in many areas they are considered to be flagship conservation species.

Start to look at yourself as an ambassador who has important knowledge to communicate. Much of this information can be spread with the help of what are probably the most charismatic birds in existence—the parrots. Your parrots or your love for parrots can take on an even greater meaning. Too many parrots have suffered at the hand of man. Some of them can now share in our reversal of those attitudes which have brought man to a critical point in his history. As a race, we have to learn again to revere nature and everything natural. We have to turn away from the consumer society which is consuming nature, leaving behind it an accelerating scale of extinctions. We MUST change. You and your birds can be part of that revolution.

Epilogue

As this book was going to press, I received news of the unfortunate little Senegal parrot featured on page 119. It seemed so appropriate to use it as an epilogue, for it is a testimony to the power of loving care. The lady who rescued the Senegal was unable to keep him permanently because her own Senegal, another male, was jealous. She writes: "I enclose a photograph of him taken with his man. He adores Jim and does not want either me or Jim's wife. He now flies very well indeed. How I missed him when he went! He is the most charismatic bird I have ever known. Once he got over his sheer terror and misery he started to talk so well and never stops playing. He is so happy. My job is well done and finished."

References

Abramson, J., B. L. Speer and J. B. Thomsen, 1995, *The Large Macaws*, Raintree Publications, Fort Bragg.

Athan, M. S., 1997, When Talking Parrots Won't Talk, *Bird Talk*, 15 (7): 20-27.

Bond, M., and K. Muser, 1997, Budgie egg production, testing procedures, metal toxicosis, *Bird Breeder*, 69 (3): 6-7.

Carpenter, S., 1997, Fagan's tale, *The Pet Bird Report*, 7 (2): 26-30.

Clubb, S. L., 1994, Life history and medical management of macaws, *Proceedings: III International Parrot Convention*, Loro Parque, Tenerife.

Cross, G., 1996, Testing for Psittacine beak and feather disease, *Australian Birdkeeper*, 9 (5): 244-245.

Csaky, K., 1997, The seven wonders of my world, *The Pet Bird Report*, 6 (6): 26-30.

Davis, C., 1997, Celebrating the Bird/Human Bond, *Bird Talk*, February: 100-101.

Greeson, L., 1996, Quaker Parrakeets: what makes them so special? *Bird Talk*, 14 (11): 106-111.

Hall, C., 1997, Familiar sights at the surgery, *Just Parrots*, Aug/Sept: 50-51.

Hamilton, J., 1997, New Life Parrot Rescue, *Just Parrots*, Aug/Sept: 38-9.

Holtby, C., 1997, Hazards in the home for pet birds, *Bird Keeper*, July: 51, 53.

James, G., 1997, Feathers for Alex, *The Pet Bird Report*, 7 (1): 52-3.

Jones, A., 1992, Avian Disease—some "new" syndromes and some new ideas on old favourites, *Avicultural and Veterinary Conference Proceedings*, 1992, London.

Jones, T., 1997, Connoisseur Conures, *The Pet Bird Report*, 6 (6): 55.

Knights, S., 1997, A good start for baby birds, *Just Parrots*, Aug/Sept: 57.

Linden, P. G. 1996, Early Avian Development: A Breeder's View of Important Behavioural Stages, A.F.A. *Annual Convention Proceedings*, 1996, 140-151. American Federation of Aviculture, Arizona.

—— 1997, Developing Curiosity, *The Pet Bird Report*, 6(6):4-9.

Low, Rosemary, 1972, *The Parrots of South America*, John Gifford Ltd, London.

—— 1997, Those perfect *Poicephalus* Parrots, *Bird Talk*, February: 64-77.

Rosano, D., 1996, Parrot play and toy preferences, *The Pet Bird Report*, 6(5): 52-55.

Sefton, D., 1995–6, Lories and Lorikeets, *Birds USA*, 94-7.

Spence, T., 1955, Breeding of the Purple-capped Lory, *Avicultural Magazine*, 61 (1): 14-17.

Tucker, K., 1996, Only dogs make good pets? *AFA Watchbird*, XXIII (6): 36-7.

Webb, P., 1997, Papa my pet Eclectus, part II, *Avizandum*, April, 11-12.

Wissman, M. A., 1996-7, The Baby Grey and PBFD: A Case Report, *The African Ark* 6 (3): 1, 3.

Wright, M., 1997, Together yet separate, *The Pet Bird Report*, 7 (2): 36-7.

AFA Watchbird is published by the American Federation of Aviculture, 3118 PO Box 56218, Phoenix, Arizona 85079-6218, U.S.A.

The African Ark is published by the African Parrot Society, PO Box 204, Clarinda, IA 51632-2731, USA

The Avicultural Magazine is published by the Avicultural Society, c/o Bristol Zoo, Clifton, Bristol BS8 3HA

Avizandum is published by David and Vera Dennison, PO Box 1758, Link Hills, Natal 3652, South Africa.

Birds USA is published by Bird Talk. See page 128 for this address and that of other avicultural publications.

The Pet Bird Report is published by Sally Blanchard, 2236 Mariner Square Drive #35, Alameda, CA 94501-1071, U.S.A.

Index

Entries in **bold** indicate illustration.